10 Steps To A Great Relationship

What every couple should know about love

Howard J. Rankin Ph.D

StepWise Press

Published by StepWise Press
PO Box 4797
Hilton Head Island, South Carolina
SC 29938-4797

(803) 842 7797

First printing, March, 1998

Copyright © 1998 Howard J. Rankin
All rights reserved

Library of Congress Catalog Card Number 97-97208
ISBN: 0-9658261-2-0

Printed in the United States

Cover design by ag2 inc., Hilton Head Island, South Carolina

Without limiting the rights in the copyright reserved above, no part of this publication may be reproduced, stored in or introduced into a retrieval system, or transmitted, in any form, or by any means (electronic, mechanical, photocopying, recording, or otherwise), without the prior written permission of the copyright owner and the above publisher of this book.

To M.J.
My wife and best friend

and to
James and Josh

Contents

Acknowledgments	6
Preface	7
Do We Need Long-Term Intimate Relationships?	13
The Dynamics of Attraction	21
The Five Stages of a Relationship	31
Step One: Communicating	57
Step Two: Accepting	68
Step Three: Committing	96
Step Four: Trusting	109
Step Five: Sharing	118
Step Six: Fighting Fair	126
Step Seven: Nurturing	134
Step Eight: Romancing	144
Step Nine: Forgiving	155
Step Ten: Understanding	167
Getting Help	179
Index	192

Acknowledgments

Many people have helped in the development of this book. The biggest contribution comes from the many clients who, over the years, have taught me about relationships and love.

Support and technical help has been graciously and willingly given by several people. Foremost among these has been David Anderson and his excellent staff at Anderson Communications Group and ag2 inc., on Hilton Head Island. So I extend heartfelt gratitude to Robin Wade, John Bowen, Kevin Courtney, Joe Bergeron, Mary Frances Blatchley and Jeff Cox each of whom, in their own separate ways, made it possible for me to complete this project.

Margaret-Anne Slawson and Shelley Steele at Access Publishers Network gave me endless encouragement and support as well as invaluable wisdom. Angela Fugate at McNaughton & Gunn ensured stress-free production.

The biggest contributors to this book, however, are the people who showed me how to love. Foremost among these have to be my parents who, consciously or otherwise, laid down the foundation of the *10 Steps*.

I want to thank my mother-in-law, Ellen, the personification of caring and tolerance, for her love and support. As you will see when reading the book, my sons Josh and James have in their unique ways not only inspired love but also have taught me invaluable lessons about the *10 Steps*.

Finally, my wonderful wife M.J., as well as putting up with my prolonged absences while I was preparing the manuscript, has made it progressively easier to follow the *10 Steps* and explore their full meaning.

Terminology

This book is about intimate relationships, including marriage. The core ideas contained herein apply to any intimate relationship of any sexual orientation.

Preface

Relationships are oxygen for the soul but everywhere people are suffocating. In a world where evolving technology allows us to do more, faster and with less effort, we are in danger of losing our perspective and our values. The cultural messages of a rapidly developing technological society conflict with the actions necessary for a loving relationship.

In a society where today's model is obsolete before you even get it out of the box, we have become the Disposable Society. We have a society where you can dispose of your marriage as easily as you can throw away last year's computer. Is it a co-incidence that in a society where leasing cars for three years at a time is the most predominant method of vehicle acquisition, we also have suggestions for the "limited term" marriage contract?[1]

On the threshold of the twenty-first century, convenience is the opium of the masses. Vast fortunes have been made by those smart and entrepreneurial enough to market extraordinary items that make life convenient (e.g. fax machines) or to market ordinary items conveniently (e.g. fast food). We have been conditioned to expect the simple. We do not expect to have to exert effort to make it work. If it is not user-friendly, we don't want it.

We are not only conditioned to expect functional convenience, we also expect it now, if not sooner. We are not only the Disposable Society, we are also the Instant Society - instant pudding, instant coffee, instant credit, instant divorce.

There is very little *convenient* about marriage or a committed intimate relationship. Marketing it would be a tough sell. All the important aspects of marriage and intimate relationships are neither disposable nor instant. On the contrary, intimate relationships are hard work. Our partners are very often not user-friendly. The valuable aspects of our relationships are not delivered instantly. The true

---

[1] At least one proposal for a limited term marriage agreement that contains a renewable annual option is before the courts

meaning and value of our relationships are only revealed or appreciated after many years. Melding lives together into an effective team while still retaining a separate identity takes patience and skill. We have to exercise restraint, perseverance and acceptance.

The requirements for love run completely counter to the mentality of today's Disposable and Instant Society. We are bombarded with messages about ease, convenience of use and control and come home to relationships that simply do not fit that mode. Utilitarianism rules the Instant Society. If a once made promise is now inconvenient, retract it - instantly. If you get bored with a commitment, break it - as soon as possible. In the Instant and Disposable Society, conveniences evolve, problems revolve, marriages dissolve.

The marketing culture is both a reflection and a manufacturer of the psychology of the masses. The successful advertiser senses the shadowy undercurrents of the contemporary psyche and brings them to the surface as tangible, seductive identities wrapped in visual images, tag lines and soundbytes. If our marketing culture has reified the convenient and the instant it is because we want it that way. We want to put out less and less effort. We do not want to have to exercise self-discipline. We have a strong urge to abandon impulse control, one of the core skills of love.

Successive generations of parents, through their own confusion and crises, have taught their children to be less and less disciplined. Each of the *10 Steps* that underpin loving action are learned, or not learned, in childhood. All learning is much easier in childhood when the foundations of our personality, thinking and behavior are encoded in our nervous systems. Learning anew as an adult requires excavating the original foundations and laying down new footings.[2]

All human beings begin with a great capacity for love. Appropriate psychological training is necessary to help that loving

---

[2] Therapy, part of the adult learning process, is like an archeological expedition. Sometimes it takes many years to find anything worthwhile, sometimes you find an artefact that will change the course of your personal history and sometimes you discover you have been digging in the wrong place.

capacity flourish and bloom. This book is, therefore, as relevant to child rearing as it is to marriage.

Love and Mass Confusion

If the predominant marketing culture has ambushed our values, it has hijacked the concept of love. At its heart, love is about acting in accordance with certain principles and values. Those values are neither sexy nor glamorous. They do not lend themselves easily to a soundbyte. In a world where attention span is only as long as the next television shot, concepts that take time to develop, like trust and forgiveness, are under-exposed. It's much easier to peddle and convey sex and romance than it is a concept like Acceptance. Sex and romance are, of course, an integral part of love but they are not love nor are they necessarily its most important components.

Not that Madison Avenue is totally responsible for the mass confusion that exists about love. People simply don't know what love is. In my role as a therapist, I have asked many what they meant when they said they loved someone, typically the person sitting next to them on the couch in my office. Only about 15% of people can give any answer at all and of those, one in ten provides an insightful reply. Most people think of love as a positive feeling. As you will see, I believe that this is incorrect. Romantic love is a Novel Erotic Attachment - a genetic trick designed to temporarily fuse people psychologically and physically for the purpose of procreation. With this fusion comes confusion. The Novel Erotic Attachment (NEA) fades and we are left with different perspectives, feelings and relationships. The positive feelings that accompany romantic love and the NEA set you up for love but they are not the same as love.

I did not write this book just to make an academic point about the erosion of important values. My main purpose was to provide insight and advice. Because most people don't know what love really is, it is no surprise to find that many are not very good at it. Worse still, being products of the Instant and Disposable Society, they do not know that they are not good at it. Most people will blame their partners for the break-up of their relationships in the same way that criminals blame their lawyers for their convictions. It's a rare person who honestly admits sharing the responsibility of a failed partnership.

The book was not just intended to be my version of love. At its core this was meant to be an informative and practical book based on my experiences working with many couples as well, of course, as my own life experience.

My own life experience is relevant. I married in my mid-twenties, just as I was starting my career and before I had reached any mature sense about myself. My own insecurity made me all too willing to see dependency as love, although such thoughts did not cross my mind at the time. Looking back, I don't think I had any idea why I or my wife were really getting married. Despite working in one of the most prestigious, academic psychiatric institutions in the world, no-one told me about relationships. I didn't really ask, but I suspect that had I done so, no-one would have given me a good definition of love or what it really entailed.

When we eventually divorced some years later, I had developed a little more insight. I fully accept my contributions to the failure of my marriage. Most of them were errors of ignorance and complete naiveté. I personally regret not having had the opportunity for some pre-marital sessions with a trained professional who could have shown us the horizon beyond the romantic myth, someone who could have spelled out what a loving relationship really entails. I would have also benefited from talking with someone who could have shed more light on the dynamics of our attraction and relationship. We may not have listened. Romance has a way of obscuring important details.

Such a session might have been beneficial in that it would at least have allowed us to compare dreams, aspirations and expectations. Frequently, I find that couples do not discuss in any depth, important goals or the compatibility of their expectations. If the subject of children is raised, for example, the topic typically extends no further than whether the partner is interested in having a family or not. Timing of family, child-rearing issues and family values are often not fully aired and when there is a disagreement, each partner silently believes that they will magically convince the other of their own point of view.

Age and romance are large factors in the critical errors people make at the beginning of their relationships. Both youth and romance confer feelings of invincibility that border on psychosis. For this reason, I believe that pre-marital counseling, a legal requirement in several states, is really beneficial and should be more widely adopted.

Practical advice is as necessary as education. Telling people what they need to do to have a good relationship is one thing, giving them the necessary skills is another. In all areas of life, simple knowledge is necessary but not sufficient to effect change which requires the practice of certain actions and behaviors. Practice and experience are the only really effective teachers. In addition to espousing a view of love and what it entails, I have, therefore, included some exercises designed to help you hone your love skills.

You will see that the some of the exercises I have included seem remarkably simple. Working together for a few minutes on a simple task can have the most powerful effect on a couple. Moreover, the principles that constitute love are fundamentally simple and crystal clear. Human beings, however, seem to have the hardest time doing the simplest things.

In writing a book about how to develop and improve any behavior, the focus inevitably falls on how to change unhelpful or maladaptive habits. Much of the text can, therefore, be consumed with the discussion of problems, transforming a book that is about love into a siren of despair. I have tried to avoid that wherever possible, citing cases and experiences that provide uplifting examples of the value of loving relationships. Every relationship has its issues and problems. Many of the cases that I have used to highlight classic problems were solid, loving partnerships. A relationship that is struggling with any of the *10 Steps* is not a bad or unloving union. It is simply a relationship that could reach greater heights.

It should also be said that volumes could be written on each of the *10 Steps*. My purpose is to provide an overall framework about love and relationships, stimulate thoughts and encourage new behaviors.

I have remarried and continue the work of developing those characteristics that allow me to be loving. The endless search for understanding and self-development that is both a function and a requirement of a good relationship, continues. I hope the ideas in this book stimulate helpful thoughts and lead you to greater love. I also hope this book serves a helpful guidepost on your walk through life. As the Danish philosopher, Soren Kierkegaard put it: "Life is best understood backward but you can only live it forward." [3]

Howard J. Rankin
February, 1998

---

[3] Soren Kierkegaard, a Danish philosopher lived from 1813-1855. His worked influenced the development of the existential movement.

Do We Need Long-Term Intimate Relationships?

As we approach the end of the millennium, the committed, long-term intimate relationship is still a predominant cultural and personal goal. There have always been critics of this norm and some cultures have opted for different relationship arrangements. Today the challenge to the predominant pattern of personal relationships is growing. Now, in an age of unprecedented freedom and global communication we are on the brink of a technological revolution that will challenge conventional ideas about every aspect of life. Questions will be raised about gender roles, family values, lifestyles and economics that have a bearing on the future thinking about relationships.

Two other factors also influence the future of relationships. The first of these has been the intrusion of the law into personal relationships. In the last decade, people have turned more to the courts to resolve their interpersonal problems. The Law itself does not have a concept of love. The Law is concerned with the viability of an agreement from a contractual rather than an emotional or psychological perspective. Theoretically any relationship arrangement put into appropriate contractual terms could be legally viable.

The second challenge to the conventional norm of long-term, monogamous relationships is the data that show people have difficulty in maintaining them. About half of all marriages end in divorce. A significant number of the remainder do not work very well. There are many other significant, committed relationships that break up before marriage vows are even taken. In short, the evidence is that we find long term intimate relationships difficult to sustain. The fall-out from this marital wreckage is that, by 1993, 30% of all parent-child family groups are maintained by single parents. This compares with a figure of just 13% in 1970, says a 1995 Census Bureau report.[4] This continuing trend will only increase the calls for a reconsideration of the wisdom of marriage.

---

[4] US Commerce Department Census Bureau. How We're Changing - Demographic State of the Nation; 1995. CB95-14, January, 1995.

Is marriage so difficult for contemporary society that we should simply scrap the idea in search of a better alternative? Or is marriage so essential that we should better learn how to make it work? Several factors inform these questions.

Biological Considerations

At a basic physiological level, we are programmed by our genes to procreate. It has been argued that the main life force on earth is the selfish gene's sole motivation to reproduce. Succinctly stated, our genes program the rest of our bodies to live our lives simply for the purpose of procreation.

Some species, like contemporary Man, have monogamous relationships. There are species in which mates pair up and stay together for the entire life-cycle (e.g. many birds, geese). Many other species, however, have no such monogamous relationships. In those species, dating and courtship last through one cycle of mating. The female produces offspring and the male disappears never to be seen again.

Biologically, we only need to have sexual intercourse to continue the species. From a purely procreation perspective, a biological view suggests that long term intimate relationships are not necessary unless they confer real biological advantages. For example, does such a relationship lead to more frequent intercourse and thus more likelihood of procreation? Does monogamy reduce the risk of sexually transmitted diseases and lead to healthier offspring and parents? Does the stability of a monogamous relationship make procreation more likely because of the psychological benefits (e.g security) that a good monogamous relationship confers?

The complexity of the human brain requires more programming and nurturing than lower species. It is possible to continue the species without parent bonding but it is not the *best* way. The presence of both parents is the best way of maximizing a child's security, performance, skills and above all, its capacity for love.

Social Considerations

There is strong evidence that marriage confers health, social, psychological and financial advantages. Togetherness and companionship are critical elements in better adjustment and performance. This is true, even in childless marriages. The decision not to have children is a reasonable one that is becoming more accepted. The motivation to marry for many, however, is a desire to have a family. From a social point of view, what advantages, if any, are conferred by a two parent compared to a single parent upbringing? In an era where mothers have careers and child care is the norm, there is considerable question of the need for marriage. Women are self-sufficient and do not need the support of a male partner, the argument goes. So how valuable, from a social viewpoint, is a two parent family?

Relevant evidence has been generated by the divorce epidemic of the past thirty years. This has focused attention on single parent families, blended families and the overall need to have two parents stay together.

The view that predominated for most of the twentieth century was that parents should stay together for the benefit of the children, no matter what. Regardless of the level of tension and dysfunction that resulted from forcing ill-suited and angry partners to live together, the family unit and the children were considered primary.

In the late sixties and seventies, however, research began to question this view. The accumulated evidence suggested that children did best in a peaceful home even if that meant being separated from a parent, typically the father. Peace and lack of tension are more critical for childhood development than the enforced illusion of unity. As a clinician, I have no doubt that those principles still hold true: I would rather see children raised in a single-parent peaceful household than in a two parent family that resembles a war zone.

Saying that single parent households are better than traumatic two parent households is, however, not an endorsement of that lifestyle in the normal course of events. Single parenting can be better than a bad alternative in dire circumstances but that does not make it the best lifestyle of choice. Unless there is an unacceptable level of stress and trauma, children need both parents.

Children need both parents for many reasons. At a basic level, children need time and attention. There are more likely to get the time and attention they need if there are two parents. Children also need to form strong attachments and relationships with both an adult male and female. These early relationships form the pattern of their relationships with men and women for the rest of their lives. As you will read, these relationships are critical in attraction, subsequent mate selection and marital adjustment.

Two parents can be mutually supportive in the difficult task of parenting. Frequently, I hear a single parent claim that parenting is easier because they do not have another adult to question and contradict their child-rearing practices. No doubt this makes child-rearing *easier* but not necessarily better. There are times when a child (not to mention children) can wear down a lone parent and erode their ability to maintain discipline.

Two parents can also model love. They can show what a loving relationship is meant to be and emphasize the importance of marriage at the center of the family. Moreover, the family is the quintessential and primary social group. A person's relationship with the world is determined by their role and experience within their family. The family experience needs to be as loving as possible for that reason. A family that fosters fractured relationships binds its children in a cast for the rest of their lives.

Some typical roles in a family	
Caretaker	**Ugly Duckling**
Peacemeaker	**Clown**
Black Sheep	**Airhead**
Victim	**Scapegoat**

You can learn much about someone's relationship capacity by understanding his/her relationships with parents and his/her role within their nuclear family.

Are Biological Parents Important?
It could be argued that children can be nurtured by any loving adult. How necessary is it for those adults to be the biological parent?

It is certainly true that many step-parents and parent figures are enormously loving and exert vastly positive influences in the lives of their children. A loving parental substitute is far better than no substitute and there are clearly many cases where surrogate parents are more loving than the biological ones. Overall, however, the ideal situation is to be raised by biological parents. In the way that sex creates attachment between two adults that primes them up for loving action, parenthood creates special feelings and attachment that makes love of the child more likely.

We crave unconditional love. Giving unconditional love is difficult and demanding. It is easier to give unconditional love to an infant. A baby is helpless, has primitive demands for physical comfort and can be completely controlled. Once babies develop into toddlers with minds of their own and bodies that cannot so easily be controlled, the delivery of unconditional love becomes more challenging. *The special bond between parent and child makes unconditional love more likely.*

There is also strong evidence to suggest that the absence of biological parents creates relationship and attachment difficulties. Such problems are more common among adoptees, children who lose parents at an early age and children of broken families who have no contact with a biological parent.

Psychological Considerations
In the last analysis, children need long-term relationships for the same reasons that adults do. All functioning human beings need security, stability and companionship.

Security meets primitive needs of survival. Security means that you are not threatened physically or emotionally. If you do not have security your survival becomes your prime concern and activity. This reduces you to a very basic level of functioning and interferes with your ability to thrive. Insecurity disrupts all facets of a relationship. It is virtually impossible to learn or practice the *10 Steps* unless you are in a situation that confers security.

Stability is predictability. All of us want control and predictability gives us the chance to exert such control. Human beings need stability. Change is stressful, volatility is unbearable. Many marital partners describe their situation as one of stability rather than one of happiness. One of the reasons that many marriages stay intact is that people opt for stability rather than the uncertain chance of increased happiness.[5]

Companionship is an essential human requirement. We need attention. We need people to listen to us. We need people with whom we can share our innermost feelings.[6] Our experience is self-contained - it is felt entirely alone within our own being. Our experience only becomes understandable and meaningful when it is shared with others.

Meaning is essential to life. You alone can find meaning in your life but you cannot find it on your own

Life is inherently a lonely experience. Except for a few months at the beginning of life, we experience life as separate beings. Our relationships are the only way we can moderate the anxiety of being alone. Our relationships are also the only way to verify and validate our realities. The way in which we make sense of our experience is through our interaction with significant others. Frequently, parents are oblivious to the fact that their interaction with the child is indeed providing the crucial function of organizing the child's experience and making it comprehensible. The biological parents are, all other things being equal, the best people to shape their child's experience. For one thing, parents share with their children genes and family history. Suppose, for example, a mother had juvenile-onset diabetes (or any

---

[5] As societal structure has become less rigid and people's lives more unpredictable, neurosis has increased. Writers like Eric Fromm argue convincingly that the price of freedom is an increase in insecurity and anxiety.

[6] Confidantes have become harder to find as society has advanced, which is why there are people like me in business

other medical condition). Her awareness of the condition, how it manifested itself in her, how to respond to it will all be enormously helpful to her offspring. More than that, her experience of the problem will allow her to understand its dimensions and effectively communicate them to her child.

Of course, no parent is ideal, because we bring to this difficult task our neuroses and issues. It is for that reason that both biological parents are necessary child-rearing.[7]

The Argument For Maintaining Relationships

Few sane people would disagree with the argument that relationships are essential. Some would argue, however, against the need to maintain the same relationship over a long period. Theoretically one could have a series of relationships with a variety of different partners and still get all of the advantages of companionship, security and stability mentioned above.

A certain amount of experimenting and developing life experience is natural and it is not uncommon for people to have had a couple of long term intimate relationships before they finally select a mate. I see four main problems, however, with a lifetime pattern of having a series of relationships as implied by the notion of the limited time marriage contract.

A constant change of partners will seem like failure. Failing at relationships will only increase your unhappiness.

A pattern of changing relationships does not confer stability. It encourages insecurity and defensiveness and inhibits the performance of many of the *10 Steps* and thus inhibits love. If you are constantly

---

[7] I am not a fan of parent-bashing. The child will only see its parents as parents rather than individuals and it is difficult for them to understand or appreciate parenting dilemmas (until they grow up and become parents themselves). In any situation, a parent can only take one action. Because there are an almost infinite number of alternatives, this leaves infinity-1 options that were not taken. In retrospect, at least one of these options will always look better than the action that was taken from a child's viewpoint. This means that virtually every parental decision can be, and often is, second-guessed

changing partners, you are either deliberately seeking instability or creating it, consciously or otherwise.

With repeated break-up of relationships commitment, one of the *10 Steps*, becomes difficult. It is difficult to have a loving relationship without *commitment*.

Switching from partner to partner also avoids the difficult but rewarding task of changing, accepting and accommodating to another person. In truth, this is why most people break up their relationships - they are not prepared to the hard work involved in maintaining them. If you are not prepared to do the hard work of maintaining one relationship why would you expect a second, a third or a fourth be any different? The evidence suggests that people expect subsequent relationships to be different but, in general, they are not. The divorce rate is higher for subsequent marriages than it is for first marriages.

There are, therefore, many compelling reasons for maintaining a stable, long-term, intimate relationship. All the evidence suggests it is the arrangement that enhances our health and well-being. It is the one that gives children the best chance of developing into loving, secure adults. It is also the arrangement that will best meet the majority of our own needs. It is the arrangement that gives us our best shot at happiness and fulfillment. It is nothing less than our best hope for the future of the human race.

As critical as these partnerships are, they often do not fulfill all of our needs. Living together provides some difficult challenges. Marriage is so important that we need to try hard to make it work.

The Dynamics of Attraction

Before considering the *10 Steps* that constitute love, it is important to have some understanding of the dynamics of attraction. Our choice of partners reveals much about who we are and how we approach relationships.

Attraction is a complex and fascinating topic. There are many levels of explanation that account for mate selection but many people are unaware of the dynamics of their relationships and the psychological factors that shape their choices.

I always ask couples how they met and what attracted them to each other. The replies are fairly predictable. People it seems are attracted by physical characteristics, or personality traits. The physical characteristics extend to virtually every part of the anatomy. Kindness, a sense of humor, strength, sexiness, are traits that are typically endorsed. Very few people, however, directly refer to the dynamics of the relationship to account for their attraction and selection.

The dynamics of the relationship refers to the way the partners' psychological needs match. He is insecure, she is strong. She is dependent, he is controlling. He needs reassurance, she is attentive. He is jealous, she is introverted. These dynamics are fundamental to understanding attraction. As we mature we understand ourselves and this process better. As a result, as people get older, they are sometimes wise enough to recognize that not everybody they find attractive would make a suitable partner.

Programmed Selection

Throughout the animal kingdom the simplistic rule of thumb is that females seek males who can be good providers and males seek females who have all the hallmarks of being able to bear children. This translates into human courtship and selection. Like many observations of the animal kingdom, however, the data generalize only to a degree. Human beings are more evolved and conscious and have thus developed other influences over their behavior, including mate selection. Nonetheless security is a factor in female mate selection, and childbearing potential a factor in the mate selection of males.

Psychological Influences

One of the biggest psychological factors in mate selection and attraction is parental similarity. Why do we seem to end up with spouses who have characteristics of one of our parents - even when we have consciously set out to specifically avoid such a scenario? The answer is in what might be called our "comfort zone."

Our parents shape our communication and therefore our thinking patterns. They may make us feel wonderful, inadequate, ashamed, guilty, tense, angry, pampered. Whatever the game that is transacted between you and your parents it becomes the foundation of your thinking. Even if you do not like the game, or the feelings that go along with it, it is the one that you know the best and *feel comfortable* playing.

Imagine that you were forced to learn to play the trombone as a child. You learnt, somewhat reluctantly, how to do this but the trombone is not your favorite instrument - you hate the sound. It is, however, the one instrument that you know how to play and if you had to chose one instrument to play if you life depended on it - the trombone would be your choice.

Let's suppose you start dating and you meet someone who metaphorically doesn't want you to play the trombone. They want you to play the violin. This is very appealing because you much prefer the violin to the trombone. The only problem is that you don't know how to play the violin. This makes you insecure. When you try to play the violin there are times when it sounds an awful lot like a trombone - and there are times when you find yourself, out of sheer force of habit, reverting to that old trombone.

Intimate relationships are challenging. They make us feel vulnerable. When someone comes along who wants you to play the trombone, you feel comfortable. You know how to do that. And there's always the chance that this partner will make you actually enjoy playing this instrument.

Whatever the particular game you played with your parents, it's a game that you want to win. You want to prove to your alcoholic dad that you can get him to stop drinking by being a perfect little girl. You want to prove to your mother you can get her attention by shocking her with outlandish boyish antics. You want to prove to your father that you are not as inadequate as you think he thinks you are. Not only do you want to prove these things to your parents, you have to prove them to yourself. Proving them to yourself is a sign of your power and your self-esteem depends on it.

One of my female clients was raised by a critical father who desperately wanted a son. This desire was directly related to his guilt about the death of his own brother. My client and her sister both went out of their way to adapt boyish habits and eschew femininity in the fruitless pursuit of their father's affection. My client grew up with confusion about her own identity, difficulty embracing feminine things, and very low self-esteem one manifestation of which was a total inability to accept a compliment or recognize her several talents and accomplishments. This created many problems until she realized the nature of her resistance. Being a boy was literally the only way she could have ever "won her father over." Because she was not a boy (and would not consider a gender change operation) she could never measure up. Nothing could ever be good enough. The bind was inescapable.

And so the beat goes on with us children trying to win unwinnable battles, caught up in the games designed by our parents and their parents before them. The game is all consuming. It permeates every aspect of our lives and our daily functioning. It is at the heart of our very survival.

The game is an obsession. Consciously we might recognize that game for what it is and try to abandon it. Even when we are consciously trying to avoid the game, however, along comes somebody who at an unconscious level reminds us in some way of our parent and we are hooked right back into the obsession.

The similarity that our partners have to our parent figure can take many forms. That similarity may be physical, it may be psychological - it can be any feature that unconsciously or consciously reminds us of that significant parent. The hook is often unconscious because consciously many of us have made up our mind to avoid parental similarities like the plague.

It takes a long time, if ever, to abandon the game of saving the parent or getting the attention we crave. Most of the time we continue with the fantasy that we can win the game. Our attraction to someone is often very strong precisely because we feel here is a person with whom we can play the game and win. In the initial stages of our relationship, when we are in the midst of the romantic infatuation, it feels very much like we have won. We feel the unconditional love of our partner and we feel unified with them in a way that almost always eluded us a children. At last, victory, peace and joy!

But wait! As the early romantic infatuation fades and separateness replaces the temporary illusion of unified love, you discover that you have not won the game at all. In fact, you are playing the game with the same frustration and the same dismal results. Just when you thought you had won, you have victory abducted from your own front door. The problem is that the game is unwinnable even with someone, who, for a while, made you feel like a winner.

There are two important ramifications of this scenario.

1. The very characteristics that attracted you to your partner will pose the greatest threat to your relationship.

2. Your partner's unwillingness to let you win will be a source of great frustration and even resentment.

At the core of this problem, however, lies your very salvation. Caught now with a partner who won't let you win the game either, it would seem that you have two main options.

⇒ Continue with the struggle and treat your partner more and more like your parent figure.

⇒ See the game for what it is and stop playing.

If you choose the first course of action, you run the risk of more anger, frustration and depression and you may eventually dissolve the relationship. If you choose the second course of action, you will be free but your spouse might be miserable.

In a truly loving marriage, however, your spouse will help you resolve this problem, if you allow it.

Katrina was raised in a chaotic household. Her father was unpredictable - seldom happy, seldom sober, seldom there. Her mother was depressed but functional. As the oldest child, Katrina took on the responsibility for cheering mother up and making life easier for her two younger siblings. At an early age she became a perfectionist. She spent much of her time cleaning and clearing up so that mother would not be faced with the evidence of her own inadequacy. This also had the added bonus of knowing that her father, coming home to a house that was neat as a pin, would have one less thing to rant about. Tidiness and order were Katrina's currency of control. This did have the short term effect of mildly moderating some of the excesses of her parents' problems. By the time Katrina went to college, however, her father had long gone and her mother was still depressed - a testimony to the child's inability to effect the long term outcome of a marriage.

College was difficult. Katrina was an excellent student but was prone to bouts of mild depression. She found it difficult to have fun and envied the easy-going nature of many of her friends. Once she tried to share an apartment with some of her fellow students but they kicked her out after six weeks because they could not stand her obsessions with tidiness.

Katrina went on to a masters and then a doctoral program. It was there that she met Frank, an intellectual equal with a great sense of humor. They dated for several months before deciding to move in together.

Despite really making a conscious effort to minimize her need for control and neatness, Katrina continued to be obsessive. She did not realize how pervasive and compulsive her behavior had become. Katrina's antennae had, however, really picked out the right guy for her. Frank *really* did not mind her obsession. Being a guy, he did not quite understand the need for total orderliness but he did not object to it either. At the beginning, Frank was really appreciative of Katrina's housekeeping. It felt to Katrina that at last here was someone who really appreciated her effort. Here was someone that gave her obsessive habit some meaning, she thought. She was wrong, of course, Frank did not really care one way or another. Her obsession had very little impact on his feelings. Very little impact, that is, until he started to realize how destructive the habit was for Katrina.

Katrina became more stressed as important exams approached. As so frequently happens at times of stress, she responded by increasing her coping behavior and her cleaning obsession led to less time spent studying, falling further behind, increased tension and even more cleaning.

It was at this point that Frank started to address his partner's obsession as a problem rather than an eccentricity. The problem was creating a strain on the relationship and Frank sought me out to help him deal with the issues. Although, of course, he had a long-term vested interest in Katrina's well-being, his main concern when we first spoke about it together, was for Katrina herself. Fortunately, Katrina had selected a mate who really did not have a problem with orderliness per se. She could have chosen someone who hated her obsession but had unconsciously overlooked this fact in the heady days of the NEA.

I saw Katrina once, initially, to meet her and understand her perspective but Frank was my client in this matter. Frank genuinely wanted to help but was completely frustrated. I asked him what he thought his options were. He had thought about the following.

⇒ Prohibit her from cleaning

⇒ Send her away to study

⇒ Hire somebody to do the cleaning

All of the above suggestions were possibilities that might prove helpful. What was noticeable to me was that his list of possibilities did not include threats to break up the relationship or even take an adversarial approach. Here was someone genuinely concerned about his partner and wanting to help her very much. We considered the options he had presented.

Prohibiting Katrina from cleaning would be difficult. She would resist mightily and besides, asserting such control was not really Frank's style. All this would do would probably increase the obsessions and create even more tension.

Sending Katrina away to study was a creative idea. Frank's sister had even offered to give up her guest bedroom for a few weeks to help out. Katrina, however, would not like the idea. It would seem like punishment and, besides, Frank felt he needed to be around to help keep her motivation going.

The idea of hiring a cleaning person had merit. The house would get cleaned and at least that would remove some of the everyday pressure to keep things clean and tidy, if not quite to Katrina's high standards. The problem is that Katrina might resent an outsider doing her work and feel usurped. Now, remember that this habit is an obsession that has tremendous meaning for Katrina. It is her coping mechanism and having a stranger come in and take over might increase rather than decrease the stress. It was the act of cleaning, making everything nice, that was the meaning of the behavior, not necessarily the end product. After much discussion, we devised a strategy and Frank went home to test it out.

Frank told his partner that he was very concerned about her. He believed that she was being distracted from her studies by unnecessary chores, including the cleaning. He reiterated to Katrina that she was the most important person in his life and that he desperately wanted her to do well in the upcoming exams. Because of this, he was willing to take over more of the chores *for the next few weeks*. This included the grocery shopping and the cleaning. He also suggested that during the time before the exams he would turn their study/den completely over to her but that *she would be responsible for cleaning it and keeping it tidy*. He added, "I know I won't do as good a job as you but I think it will take the pressure off you and allow you to pass your exams with flying colors."

Consider what has happened here. Frank has offered to help. He has not criticized his mate, indeed he has praised her. He values her cleaning, except that right now she is doing too much of it. He is prepared to make the sacrifice, for a few weeks, to help her out. The plan calls for Katrina to do some cleaning - in the environment where she is going to spend the most time and where she needs to feel the most comfortable. She gets to indulge her coping behavior within limits that don't interfere with her life. There has been no confrontation. There has been no criticism - just a genuine offer of help.

The plan worked. Katrina kept her cleaning within reasonable limits. For a few weeks she learned to moderate her obsession and for the first time, tried to exert some control. It was not that her cleaning and tidying were bad - it's just that they were excessive. By his loving intervention, Frank had enabled Katrina to break the pattern. During her pre-exam time, Katrina began to accept that the house did not always have to be in pristine condition. Katrina never became sloppy and indifferent in her housekeeping but she was eventually able to accept the idea of a once a week housekeeper. Within two years Katrina had a baby daughter and with the start of her family and the demands of her children, her perfectionist criteria changed even more.

In this case, Frank showed how a loving spouse can help change a partner's unhelpful habit. He did not vent his frustration on his mate, neither did he get angry with her. There was no confrontation and criticism, merely concern and caring.

This is one example of how marriage can get you to face the issues that need to be resolved for your personal growth.

It is much more exciting to believe that you can play the game and win rather than simply give it up. It takes a long time and much maturity and self-discovery to be able to stop playing. Its a lesson often learned the hard way.

> **The Dynamics of Your Parent Relationships**
>
> Role with father (e.g. caretaker, clown):
> ....
>
> I tried to get his attention by
> ....
> ....
>
> Role with mother:
> ....
>
> I tried to get her attention by:
> ....
> ....

Physiological Attraction

An alternative view of attraction is that it is mainly physiological. In the "new age" much has been made about the sense of smell and its impact on behavior, especially mate attraction. There is no question that smell is an important sense that can trigger associations and memories. It remains to be seen how important smell and other chemicals are in mate selection and attraction. One radical view is that hormones not only increase our readiness to find and attract a mate but that attraction itself is merely a function of this hormonally induced arousal. During a period of such arousal we will find many people attractive and that apart from this biological process, mate selection is almost random. In many of his plays, Shakespeare used a simple dramatic device to create attraction between unlikely characters. Some fairy or impish character would put love potion in a drink or on the eyes of a sleeping person and the first character seen on waking would instantly become a love object.

At a primitive level, hormones do influence our readiness to attract and be attracted. Studies show that pheromones, sensitive smell related hormones, do influence mate attraction. Unfortunately we don't know as much about the physiology of attraction and the role hormones play in human beings. It says something about the human consciousness that while we don't fully understand the chemistry of attraction in our own species, we have a very clear picture of how these chemicals influence mating behavior in the fruit fly.

Human beings are, of course, more complex than the fruit fly. Hormones and pheromones obviously do play a part in mate attraction but their role is likely to be substantially less influential in a sophisticated, conscious species like man than an instinctive simple creature like the fruit fly. Research has shown that in higher species, female sexual motivation is largely independent of hormones.[8] These chemicals may have an impact on *readiness* for mating and attraction but whether they really influence our *choice* of mate seems less likely.

Other psycho-social factors are an influence on mate selection and marriage. People get married for all sorts of reasons; in order to leave home, leave town, leave insecurity behind. These are not typically good reasons for making what should be a lifetime commitment. There is research, for example, that shows that nonblack children of alcoholics are more likely to marry and marry younger than children of non alcoholic parents. One interpretation: They just want to leave a tense parental home as soon as possible. The children of alcoholics are also more likely than the matched nonalcoholic counterparts to have increased marital distress.[9] One interpretation: They take dysfunctional roles into marriage and may select inappropriate partners.

Whatever reasons people have for mate selection and attraction, the relationship voyage takes them through uncharted, difficult waters.

---

[8] In article in Neuroscience Biobehavioral Review 1990;14(2):233-241 entitled "Desire and ability: hormones and the regulation of female sexual behavior" Wallen states "Because primate females can mate without hormonal input, female sexual initiation, not copulation, is argued to be the only valid indicator of female sexual motivation."

[9] Dawson DA, Grant BF, Harford TC Parental history of alcoholism and probability of marriage Journal of Substance Abuse 1992;4(2):117-129

The Five Stages of a Relationship

In the development of a typical intimate relationship there are five distinct stages, each of which brings its own special challenges and requirements. Relationships, like the people that make them, change with time. It is inevitable that both partners will age and change, and the dynamics of their association oscillate to the pulse of these changes. Specific life events occur in the course of a relationship and these also influence the patterns of interaction. In addition, the relationship itself has predictable milestones that mark the transition from one stage of the interpersonal odyssey to another.

Even the best relationships do not fall easily into these stages. For one thing, this categorization implies that couples have children and that their marriage involves raising a family. A minority of couples do not follow this path for various reasons. It is a perfectly acceptable and reasonable decision to eschew parenthood. There are many reasons for such a course of action. Some couples simply do not want the demands of parenthood, others wish to pursue other ambitious, still others are infertile.

Regardless of parenting choices, the first three stages apply to all relationships. The way a childless couple compensates for their lack of children will determine much about the later course of their relationship and because of the innumerable variations I do not discuss that situation further. Suffice to say that many of the issues of Stage 5 are relevant to couples who have not raised a family.

Despite the limitations of any categorization there is value in conceptualizing relationships as a phased process with distinct stages. First, it does reveal what sorts of challenges are presented in the course of a relationship and the order in which they typically occur. Secondly, this categorization helps identify what the issues that occur at certain stages are really about. Third, because the model predicts that it is best to progress smoothly from one stage to the next, any difficulties can be traced to a stage that was missed, shortened or some way skipped over.

The five stages of an intimate relationship are:

- Stage 1: Initial Attraction, Early Dating and the Novel Erotic Attachment (NEA)

- Stage 2: Dating and Beyond the Novel Erotic Attachment

- Stage 3: Commitment and Co-Habitation

- Stage 4: Marriage and the Family

- Stage 5: Beyond Child-Rearing

Stage 1: Initial Attraction and Early Dating and the Novel Erotic Attachment

We are genetically and psychologically programmed to seek out mating partners. This desire is mediated through hormones and other biochemicals that increase the attractiveness of potential partners and lead us to find them and establish physical and psychological relationships. This desire, while mediated by hormones, is also strongly influenced by psychological needs. The result of this drive is a strong urge, particularly in the first half of life, to pursue intimacy and sex. [10]

As a result of this natural and strong urge, the early stages of a relationship are controlled by these hormonally driven, physical feelings. This early stage of the relationship is also dominated by feelings of high arousal - not just sexual but a general level of excitement. Which brings us to a critical point about human nature...

Whenever a physical system is running at abnormally high or abnormally low levels it will dominate behavior.

---

[10] In cases where there is no such drive, something is amiss with this mechanism, either at the physical, hormonal level or at the psychological one. Strong emotions (which are also driven by hormones) that occur as a result of specific powerful experiences, for example, sexual abuse, bad sexual experiences etc., can turn off the physical mechanism by inhibiting the production of sex hormones.

For example, if you have a strong craving for cheesecake to the point where you are experiencing physical reactions (e.g salivating), it is going to be very difficult to talk or even think yourself out of eating it. Or, if you are depressed and simply cannot get moving, it is going to be difficult to talk or think yourself out of this mood state.[11] While you have a strong desire for sex and are in the throes of a Novel Erotic Attachment, rationality will not be your strongest asset.

What happens to your rational drive when you under such fierce psychological control? Is the logical part of your brain totally immobilized? Rationality does not disappear completely. You cleverly use it to justify the actions you are taking - or rather your unconscious mind does. In order to keep a reasonable consistency between actions and thoughts, you either have to change actions or change thoughts. When you are enjoying the thrill of the Novel Erotic Attachment your strong feelings and thoughts have to be justified. Consequently, you only see the most positive aspects of your partner, are completely blind to any shortcomings (unless they threaten you) and are completely selective in your perception.

The mind will not tolerate too much difference between your actions and your beliefs.

The early stages of an intimate relationship, therefore, are characterized by a completely positive bias towards your partner. He or she can do nothing wrong. Even if your friends point out potential problems, you dismiss them. Traits that are annoying to others, are charming idiosyncrasies to you. As your relationship develops, your view of these traits can change as you have to learn to deal with them. Those charming idiosyncrasies can, over time, mature like good wine or ferment like stale beer.

In the throes of the Novel Erotic Attachment it is very difficult to accept criticism of your partner. If you are faced with someone in

---

[11] This is not to say that techniques like cognitive therapy that are designed to help you be positive and rational are not helpful - they can be extremely valuable. There are specific moments, however, when physiology will dominate and those psychological techniques will not be of much use.

this situation don't expect them to react objectively or listen to reason - they simply can't, as many a frustrated parent whose child has hooked up with an inappropriate partner will attest.

All of this means that in the initial stage of an intimate relationship, we wander blissfully around in something akin to a hormonal fog. *At this stage we cannot be objective about our partner or our relationship.*

Some writers have compared this infatuated state to a psychosis. For example, Scott Peck in The Road Less Traveled[12] describes how infatuation allows the person to suffer the illusion that the one-ness and unconditional love that we all seek, has been found. In this state, there is a regression to an infant state of attachment to mother in which, because of the undeveloped cognitive abilities of the baby, the child sees itself literally as unified with its mother. This is the essence of security and joy and is unconditional. Peck, for example, talks about the "collapse of ego-boundaries" as the two partners temporarily bond. This is followed by the reinstatement of ego boundaries once the romantic infatuation (the NEA, in my terms) wears off and a semblance of reality returns.

If it is not possible to think clearly about your partner or your relationship during this initial stage, it follows that hasty decisions and long-term plans made on the basis of a NEA are a risky proposition. It is precisely at this stage, when clarity is low and hormones are high, that many couples do make long-term commitments. It does not mean that such a relationship is doomed to failure. All of the best relationships have to pass through this attachment phase. It is just that making the biggest decision you are going to make in life would be better based on more than sexual compatibility or infatuation. The inability to clearly see the relationship is one of the reasons why the very attributes that seemed attractive at the start of the relationship are often the biggest problems later on. This inability to effectively evaluate your relationship leads me to endorse the concept of pre-marital counseling in general and especially for those couples who have dated less than a year.

---

[12] M. Scott Peck, The Road Less Traveled, Simon and Schuster, 1978.

> **A Novel Erotic Attachment can severely damage your eyesight.**

Romance or the NEA is not love in its truest sense. The NEA is a feeling and an attitude but behaviorally it does not prepare a couple very well for the real tests of their relationship. Any relationship is great while it is fun and things are going well - the real test is how the couple manages the more mundane aspects of life, shares their tasks, resolves conflict and enmeshes their lives together.

The NEA typically lasts from three to six months. Under circumstances where the couple do not see much of each other, as in a long distance relationship, the NEA will be protracted and can last several years. Eventually, however, the novelty wears off, the scales fall from your eyes and reality comes into sharper focus. At which point there is need for another psychological shift. Now your behavior is moderated and what you lose in passion you gain in a clearer vision of your partner and the relationship.

Each part of the Novel Erotic Attachment - novelty, eroticism and the attachment - are crucial to understanding the development to relationships in general and yours in particular.

Novelty

Human beings are eminently adaptable. We got to be the dominant force on this planet by being able to quickly adapt to circumstances. But the flip side of this adaptability is boredom. We are excited about our new car. It smells like a new car, it feels like a new car, it drives like a new car - for about six months. Then we get used to it. Its novelty fades like the morning mist. Even if we spray it with new car smell, we will not deceive our minds that it is new. The novelty has worn off.

The novelty wears off most things that we acquire. We buy a new house. For weeks or even months we are obsessed with the details and excited by the novelty. Within a year, however, that novelty has worn off. That's not to say we want to move, or no longer like our house, just that the excitement has evaporated. The erosion of novelty and loss of excitement is one of the main forces behind a consumer society. We get bored and want new houses, cars, computers, furniture, despite the fact that, most of the time, the possessions we have already are perfectly serviceable. This drive for newness which comes from our inherent ability to adapt quickly, also influences our relationships.

A relationship is different from a material purchase, I can hear you protest. In many ways, of course, it is. It is a dynamic, ever-changing, interactive process. But in one respect there is a similarity between a relationship and material possessions. The pursuit of both is influenced by our human nature. And the drive for stimulation and excitement is an essential part of being human.

Although there are a few whose nervous systems and early experience dictate the avoidance of stimulation, most people like excitement. They like the stimulation they get from novelty. Some people spend a vast amount of their energy and time in the pursuit of novelty and the stimulation it generates. Compulsive shoppers, gamblers, and sex addicts are fine examples of stimulation seekers. Often, people with these lifestyles are considered as having some form of addiction. At the problem end of the spectrum, people pursue stimulation to avoid their own thoughts and feelings. If you cannot tolerate the quiet of our own thoughts and mind then you will urgently avoid that situation. The more you want to avoid it, the more you will seek other ways of occupying it. The more powerful those other sources of stimulation are, the more effective they are as a distraction from your self-generated thoughts.

> **Any compulsive behavior is a defense against painful thoughts.**

The more a person is in need of distraction, the less they are able to resist the desire to seek it. In short, troubled people have poorer impulse control. The worse the impulse control, the more likely that a person will get bored easily.

Seeking stimulation and novelty is a natural human attribute. It is one of the main driving forces of attraction. Boredom signals the death throes of any activity - including a relationship. One of the real challenges in the early stages of a relationship is to maintain stimulation, interest and curiosity once the novelty - the new car smell - has worn off.

Erotic

Not only is a relationship fueled by novelty, it is also driven by sex. It is necessary for a person to be a target for erotic energy for an intimate relationship to develop. This does not necessarily mean that the partners have sex, merely that they want to. Remember that one of the key factors in attraction is the genetically programmed drive to procreate.

How a person becomes a target for erotic and sexual desires is dependent on a number of factors. We have already seen how personal experience, self-image, family dynamics and parental behavior all influence mate selection.

Attachment

Attachment is the formation of a bond with another person. In early life this attachment is programmed to be with our mothers and how this attachment is managed by both parents is crucial for healthy development. *It will also determine how well the child will manage attachment throughout its life.* If there is ever a more compelling case for the complete involvement by a mother with its child, this is it.

> **Inadequate parenting leads to inadequate attachment. Inadequate attachment leads to a history of damaged relationships.**

Proper attachment in childhood will create a sense of security in the child. From this secure base, that child will go out into the world more independently because of the reassuring knowledge that its key attachment (to its mother) is safe. If this key attachment does not feel safe the child will be spending all of its time and energy trying to make it more secure. In short, good attachment leads to both independence and nurturing. These are two of the *10 Steps* that are central to a good relationship.

The NEA is not love. It is a complex psychological state that generates very positive feelings that **encourage partners to act lovingly**. If they have not formed an attachment during this stage, it is unlikely that they ever will. Once the NEA fades, it is important that sufficiently loving behaviors have begun to survive the erosion of novelty and excitement that have characterized the first few months of the relationship.

The NEA is not just a perceptual problem. In the NEA people act differently. The psychological and physical fusion that takes place and the powerful feelings that are produced temporarily suppress neurotic[13] defenses and sensitivities, at least in relation to your beloved. When you have achieved the ultimate state there is no need for such defensiveness. As a result, people act differently when they are in the NEA. It is not that love conquers all, rather the NEA disguises all. When the NEA is over, characteristic defenses return, often to the surprise and chagrin of the respective partners.

Stage 2: Dating And Beyond The Novel Erotic Attachment

After a time, typically between three and six months, the novelty of the NEA begins to erode. The desire for complete and total togetherness begins to wear off as individuality and individual needs resurface. This is a critical moment in the relationship.

This reduction in the intensity of feeling and the need for separation can be threatening. In many ways, it is the first true test of the relationship that, up to this point, has largely been rolling along quite happily in a type of psychotic haze. Although this reduction in NEA intensity is a developmental milestone, that does not mean that both partners reach this stage at exactly the same time. One is likely to demonstrate signs of reducing the intensity before the other and this can create real problems for both parties.

Suppose that Angela has been dating Bob for four months. They have been having a great time, have been intimate and developed a closeness typical of people sharing a NEA. Then one Tuesday

---

[13] Throughout this book, I use the term neurotic to describe overly sensitive reactions that are a function of past experiences rather than logic.

evening, Angela decides that she would much rather stay at home on her own to catch up with her personal affairs and relax by herself - do a little reading, watch some television. She would also like to go out with her friends the following night, too. She has been seeing Bob virtually every day for a month but now genuinely feels as if she would like to do some other social activities with other people. She feels that the week-end will be soon enough to see Bob again.

If she has been well schooled in the romantic love myth, these feelings might be very distressing to her. She might believe that the change in the intensity of her feelings means that she no longer "loves" Bob. This could set off a whole series of uncomfortable thoughts:

⇒ This always happens to me. Is there something wrong with me that I can't sustain my love for somebody?

⇒ I am confused. I thought I loved this guy, but now I don't know.

⇒ How do I handle this?

How she handles this is of the utmost importance.

Concealing the Shift

Often in this situation, the person will attempt to conceal the shift in the intensity of feelings. So Angela might start making excuses for why she cannot see Bob for the next three nights. A friend in need, a family crisis, a physical ailment and all manner of phantom conditions are invoked to defend her absence from Bob's company and bed. There are several problems with taking this approach.

First, unless Angela is an award winning actress - and probably even if she is - she will not be able to convince her partner that these are genuine or sufficient excuses. The reason for that is....

Once you have shared a NEA, the fear of rejection is so strong that nearly everybody is ultra sensitive to the possible signs of it.

In sharing an intimate relationship, we put everything important about ourselves on the line and become highly vulnerable. As a result, we are heavily invested in the relationship and the possibility of rejection is an ever present fear.

So even if Angela had some legitimate grounds for not being able to see Bob until the week-end, chances are he will still be sensitive to the possibility that this really means rejection.

Let's consider the options available to Angela. One scenario has her thinking and acting as follows.

Angela thinks, " I would really like to spend time on my own and with my friends, but I don't want to hurt him. I won't say anything and perhaps I can keep the evenings short." So, Angela goes out on her date but as the evening wears on, her unease begins to surface. Bob senses this immediately and seeing that their evening is not one of complete bliss, asks his partner what is wrong. She says she has a head ache (which she probably does have, brought about by the conflict she finds herself in) - he doesn't quite believe it and they find themselves squarely in the "You are holding something back/fear of rejection" game.

The problem with taking this defensive position is that Angela. does not have anything to be defensive about. While she may genuinely not to want to hurt her partner, she is short changing herself. **She is setting up a dangerous pattern by denying or not expressing her feelings.** Moreover, she has shortchanged Bob by not giving him a chance to honestly respond to how she feels.

She has also made the most common communication mistake - she has assumed she knows how Bob is going to react. ***This assumption of how someone is going to react is known as <u>projection</u> and is the biggest destroyer of relationships.***

Another danger with this approach is that Angela's defensiveness now becomes the focus of the discussion rather than her feelings about the relationship.

Ways to effectively communicate the reduction in infatuation that inevitably occurs...

1. Recognize that it is inevitable to begin with. Talk about the different stages of a relationship with each other.

2. Be as honest as possible with yourself as well as your partner.

3. Focus on the positive aspects of the relationship you are looking forward to developing. For example, I am looking forward to knowing you more, meeting your family, you teaching me tennis.

Addressing the Shift
Angela can handle this situation in other ways.

Let's suppose Angela decides that it is important she talk to Bob about how she feels. Being a sensitive soul she decides that this would be best done face-to-face and she arranges to meet Bob in private. When they meet she says the following:

"I'm having a great time with you, Bob, but you're wearing me out! I have got to have some time to catch up with the rest of my life. I have to balance my checkbook, call my grandmother, wash my hair, write in my journal, rotate the tires, finish my term paper, mend my clothes, clean out my closet[14] and if I don't get them done I am going to start feeling out of control. We have been having such a good time that it is inevitable that we would need a little bit of a break. But I can't wait until we're together again at the week-end..."

What happens next is really important. Bob can react in a number of ways. If he says..

"You know what, I was beginning to feel a bit that way myself. I am so glad we have the sort of relationship where we can talk about these things. I read this book by a guy called Rankin and

---

[14] Choose any three of these

he said that this is inevitable and does not mean we don't care for each other or have a good relationship," the two of them have established a tremendous basis for honest communication and shown respect for each other's feelings.

Suppose Bob does not react like that. Suppose he says..

"I knew it. I was just waiting for this to happen. I knew this wasn't going to last. I bet you're going to see that guy[15] again."

The significance of this message depends on how long Bob maintains this position. If, for example, after a few minutes Bob gets his act together, apologizes and confides that his reaction only stems from a genuine desire to maintain the relationship, and if he validates and recognizes Angela's need for a little space, then his insecurity about abandonment and rejection is under some control. If, however, he continues to rant and rave for a few hours or even days, his insecurity is out of control and Angela has just been given a great big warning sign.

Bob might react in other ways. He might, for example, look very hurt and burst into tears. He might wholeheartedly agree with but in a compliant, obsequious way.

The critical elements in assessing this first test of the relationship are

- How easy is it to talk about how you feel?
- Are your feelings understood?
- Are your wishes respected?
- Is your partner forthcoming about their own feelings?
- Is there a sensible discussion and an agreement about what to do next?

---

[15] Angela's last boyfriend

- Are your partner's reactions appropriate in both content and intensity?

WARNING!

Some people never get beyond the ending of the NEA. As soon as this phase begins to fade they find some way of ending the relationship. These are people who have multiple marriages, each of which only lasts a few months. If you are the sort of person who does not get beyond the NEA phase you need to recognize that romance and love are not the same. You need to realize that the euphoric feelings of the early stage of the relationship cannot be maintained and that chasing those feelings, and only those feelings rather than a meaningful relationship, is going to perpetuate your problem.

The reduction in the intensity of the NEA, therefore, focuses on several key issues of a relationship.

⇒ **Communication.** As you already have seen above, the communication patterns that were established around this sensitive issue are fundamental. In Step 1, which specifically covers the topic, you will discover other essentials of good communication.

⇒ **Independence.** Another key issue is the balance between independence and time spent together. A healthy relationship is one in which both parties have independence (i.e. function healthily as separate people). In Step 7, which covers this subject in detail, you will discover the difference between love and dependence.

⇒ **Trust.** How comfortable are the partners with trusting the other person with their feelings? The NEA is a powerful force and arouses intense feelings. Has your partner handled them with respect?

Let us suppose that Angela and Bob overcome the crisis of the reduction in their NEA and the emergence of their separateness and individuality and have now settled into a stable dating relationship. The key issue is about to become the level and nature of the commitment they make to each other.

Can I Date Other People?

If the relationship continues beyond the NEA the question of dating other people inevitably arises. This discussion is really about trust and commitment, as well as an indication of intensity of feelings.

The complexities of this question include..

- What does "date" mean? Where does sex fit into this picture, especially in view of AIDS and other sexually transmitted diseases?

- If dating others is agreed upon, how much information is to be shared about the nature of those relationships?

- Under what circumstances will such "dating" be agreed on? (for example, one partner might be going overseas for six months)

Many people are frightened of commitment. In the chapter on commitment, fears that underpin the difficulty to commit are discussed. Briefly, these include…

- Fear of rejection

- Fear of loss of independence

- Fear of loss of excitement

- Fear that they cannot maintain a commitment to one person (i.e. they will be unfaithful)

- Fear that their partner may not be able to maintain the commitment to them (i.e. their partner will be unfaithful)

- Fear of making a wrong decision

Making a commitment is not a moral obligation - being honest to your partner is. You may decide for all sorts of reasons that you cannot make a commitment. If you decide that you cannot do this you must…

⇒ Be honest with your partner and explain why you cannot commit

⇒ Be fair - don't expect them to commit to you if you are not prepared to do the same

⇒ Be honest with yourself. Is this a recurring problem for you? Is it always difficult to commit to someone else? If it is, you need to address this, otherwise you might deprive yourself of a great relationship. Perhaps you have a problem committing to anything, not just personal relationships?

I Need Some Time On My Own

Even if you and your partner agree not to date other people, the issue of independence is still unresolved. Committing to someone does not mean owning them, neither does it mean controlling them. The discussion about independence also becomes a discussion about the power struggle within the relationship.

> **A healthy relationship is where both partners not only have fulfilling lives and identities outside of the relationship, but actively encourage each other to do so.**

Take the case of Steven and Carol, a young couple I saw at just this stage of their relationship. Their relationship had developed through the novel erotic attachment stage and as they entered the second stage, they moved in together (stage 3), on Steven's suggestion. Note that they were effectively skipping a stage which often creates problems..

Stage 3: Commitment and Co-Habitation

Carol had been turned on by Steven's intensity. He was always very attentive and wanted to spend all of his time with her. Carol admitted that no-one had ever wanted her around so much and she was flattered by this attention. Although she was a little hesitant about moving in with Steven after they had known each other less than six months, she was convinced that he was her Mr. Right. Once they moved in together, however, a familiar story emerged.

Almost immediately after they started to live together, Steven's interest in going out and having a fun time with Carol almost completely evaporated. He was content to stay at home and watch television. He would overrule Carol's objections to their lack of social life by claiming they needed to save money for their dream home. He would find ways of sabotaging any outside social activities by coming home late from work or developing mild physical ailments that prevented them from going. What was worse, he was adamant that Carol not go out without him. He got angry and defensive when she talked about going out with some of her girl-friends for lunch. Carol felt imprisoned. In literally a few days she had gone from feeling very much loved to feeling trapped and possessed.

When stage 2 is shortened and you go from the NEA to living together, there has often not been enough preparation for the generally difficult task of melding your lives together in a satisfactory way. This is especially true if this is your first experience of living with someone.

Another problem that comes from missing the stage of dating from separate homes is that it is more difficult to establish the separateness and need for independence that typifies the end of the NEA. In the first example above, Angela had a difficult enough time separating from Bob even while having a separate apartment. Imagine how much more difficult that would have been if they had already moved in together.

The issue of separateness is really one of control and this is the central problem that needs to be resolved when a couple begins co-habiting. As Carol in the example above discovered, Steven's vision of a life together was quite different from hers. Before co-habiting it is important to have an understanding about what life on a daily basis is going to be like. Typically couples think they know their partners because they have spent a week on vacation together or spent a few nights together.If these times together have been spent during the NEA they will not translate very well to a post NEA, everyday existence. Being on vacation together is not the same as living together.

Some questions to discuss and resolve before co-habitation

What is the monthly budget?
How much does each party contribute?
What will the social/entertainment schedule and budget be?
How much time will be spent in separate activities?
What are the typical daily schedules?
How are the household chores going to be divided?
What is the policy for houseguests and visitors?
Where will the holidays be spent?
What will a typical weekend be like?
Will the toilet seat be left up or down?

When you co-habit all aspects of your life become public. Actions, even trivial ones, that you have been used to doing in complete privacy, now become visible and subject to your partner's appraisal. Similarly, you now have to deal with the different way your partner acts. This period of adjustment can be difficult and the more stable you are as a couple the easier it will be.

Co-habiting does, however, shift the emphasis of the relationship from social dating more towards the management of everyday tasks and chores. Who is going to do the cooking? Who is going to take the trash out? Who collects the dry cleaning?

These questions inevitably require delegation. This delegation is not only about giving up control and responsibility it is about the ability to accept that your partner will not necessarily do the task the same way you would - or even have the same standards. Sharing your life typically requires accepting different standards. This is not necessarily a bad thing - it's just different and requires an adjustment.

Not only does co-habiting require decisions about the deployment of time, it also involves decisions about money and its control. Many couples, even in an advanced stage of co-habitation, still have not worked out how to resolve the issue of money. Sometimes, after I have been a silent witness to a heated dispute about how money should be divided, I can stand it no longer. I ask them to calculate their expenses and derive an equitable way for their division. Then I get both parties to agree to the plan and encourage them to stage regular financial meetings.

I am, however, not that naïve. Money is about power. Compromising over money is about trust and sharing, two of the *10 Steps*. If one partner is angry with the other it will be difficult for them to share. If one partner can't give up control, or cannot trust, or is suspicious or simply is not good at sharing, the money issue will be a continuous thorn in the side of the relationship.

The underlying principle here is one of perceived fairness. If you believe that there is an inequitable distribution of any resources, anger and resentment are likely to be your companions. Your belief may be completely grounded in reality or a function of an unreasonable view of fairness, or both. This topic is discussed more fully in Step 5, on sharing. Suffice to say that as you learn to intertwine your lives, sharing becomes a key behavior.

Stage 4: Marriage and Child Rearing
The arrival of children is a rite of passage that transforms the marital relationship. Starting a family creates even more challenges that simple co-habitation. For one thing, having children is one of the few irreversible actions in life. You can't send them back - as much as you might periodically desire to do so. You can't really even divorce them. You might walk out and remove yourself from all contact but they will always be your children. You can disown them but you cannot disown history and genetics. They might not like it, you might not like it, but they will always be yours.

There is evidence that having a family enhances marital stability even as it imposes more strains on the marriage itself. The development of a family is one of the true joys in life and even when it is not, people stay committed to their marriages because of children.

One study sheds light on these dynamics. In a summary of the research the author states the findings like this.

"Net of controls for age at marriage, year of marriage, education, and marital duration, (marital) stability increases with family size up to the third child but starts to decline as family size reaches five or more children. Aging of children is disruptive until the youngest child reaches adulthood, after which marriages become much more stable. Arrival and aging of children is an important dynamic with strong implications for marital stability."

Heaton (1990)[16]

The arrival of children also changes the dynamic of relationships and you go from being a partnership to being a family. A two person relationship is called a dyad. A couple is one dyad. The arrival of the first child creates three dyads because three people can be divided into three sets of twos - mother-father, mother-child, father-child. The arrival of a second child creates a grand total of six dyads. The arrival of a third child creates a total of ten dyads. The dynamics of the home just got geometrically more complicated.[17]

In addition, the first child's arrival also creates a threesome - and three can be a problematic number because one member of the threesome can feel or be made, the odd man out. In fact, a threesome allows for all sorts of games, like one member playing the other two members off against each other.

So even though the arrival of children might increase marital *stability* some studies show that marital *happiness* declines, particularly with the arrival of the first child.[18] There are clearly vast individual differences here but the potential is that the enormous

---

[16] Heaton, T.B., Marital stability throughout the child-rearing years. Demography 1990 Feb;27(1):55-63
[17] If a couple have ten children, there are 66 dyads!
[18] Dalgas-Pelish PL The impact of the first child on marital happiness. Journal Adv Nursing 1993 Mar;18(3):437-441

changes brought about by a first born can impact the contentment within the marriage.

The changes in dynamics are compounded by the fact that each partner now has a different and heretofore untested and thus unknown role, namely being a parent. No matter how much talking has been done, how many classes have been attended, how many hours have been spent baby-sitting, there is no adequate preparation for parenthood - unquestionably the greatest challenge of your life. If your spouse stretched you, your children will put you on The Rack.

First, there is an increase in chores, many of which you would never have envisaged yourself doing until your infant arrived. Increased sleeplessness, financial obligations, difficulty in arranging social arrangements are some of the price you have to pay for the wonder of having brought your progeny into the world. More importantly than simply having to do more, however, are five other more significant challenges to your relationship.

1. **You have to develop teamwork** Working together as a team is essential to good parenting. Children have a special and different relationship with each parent and wherever possible will use this fact to their best advantage. Being divided as a couple over child care issues allows the child to exert control over its parents and radically interfere with the marital relationship. Giving a child such control is bad for all parties. The child has a dangerously inflated sense of its own power and this will erode respect. The parents are divided and the one partner who is the odd person out will feel angry with the other two members of the triangle. This might lead to increased and unreasonable effort by the odd person out to reassert power, thus risking the polarization of the alignment. There is a body of research showing the detrimental effect of divided parents on the behavior of their children. In one study, parental disagreements over child-rearing was a factor in the development of behavior problems in sons. Such arguments over child-rearing were a better predictor of these problems than overall marital adjustment.[19] Working together not

---

[19] Jouriles EN, Murphy CM, Farris AM, Smith DA, Richters JE, Waters E Marital adjustment, parental disagreements about child rearing, and behavior

only protects against such 'splitting' but is necessary to establish appropriate family and child rearing values. Too often, the important business of setting priorities and establishing values happens by default, if at all. Parents do have to respond to the specific challenges presented by each unique child at the time they are happening. No amount of planning can prepare a parent for every situation they will face. The more prepared a parent is, however, the more confident they will be in their decision-making and the more appropriate those decisions will be. Establishing a process for learning about child development is important. There are many good sources of information on every stage of child development and parents need to educate themselves if they are going to be able to make the best child-rearing decisions. Moreover, parents need to work out between them how to enforce such decisions. You may have an encyclopedic knowledge of what is best for your child but if you cannot enforce these principles such knowledge is useless.

2. **You have to consciously establish family values**. The discussion of child-rearing practices inevitably includes a discussion of family values. Whatever action you take has an implied meaning. Each person will derive their own meaning from the event, and this will be the most influential aspect of the encounter. For example, I was counseling a teenage girl who was beginning the difficult process of reuniting with her father after a number of years. She had just been to see him for the first time. During the weekend visit, her father had been furtively smoking pot. When his daughter confronted him about this he did confirm that he had indeed been smoking it. "I am not going to lie her," he told me, proud of his honesty. His daughter on the other hand was upset. She did not like or condone pot-smoking. Her father had not even considered how his behavior might affect her. He saw himself as honest, she saw him as selfish and inconsiderate. Children are particularly good at letting you know their interpretation of your actions and when you have violated some moral principle. Parental unity can be stretched to the limits when this happens.

---

problems in boys: increasing the specificity of the marital assessment. Child Development 1991 Dec; 62(6):1424-1433

The arrival of children therefore, requires communication, acceptance, and understanding. Moreover, as these important issues surface there is a danger that the identities of the partners get subsumed under the weight of their parenting obligations. This change presents special challenges to the couple just staring out their family.

3. **You have to adapt to changing roles**. With the arrival of the child, roles and behavior change. In the early stages of childhood this specifically means that the wife now has another focus for her time, energy and affection. The insecure or possessive man can be threatened by the typical dilution of attention that he thus experiences. Communication and nurturing are critical, otherwise resentment can easily set in. The man needs to understand the strong biological needs that a woman has to nurture and protect her infant. This will change the marital relationship, especially in the early stages of parenting.

4. **You have to preserve the prominence of the marriage**. As children develop and become a central focus in the family there is a danger that the partners' first priority becomes the children rather than each other. This is hardly surprising since so much of the time revolves around the management of the children. The elevation of the child over a spouse again gives the child too much power and divides the marriage. Sometimes, of course, a child's needs to have priority. Overall, however, the child and the relationship will flourish most in an environment where it is clear that the marital relationship is strong and underpins everything else. Not that it is easy resisting the demands of your adorable child. Recently, my wife and I were discussing how to spend some upcoming free time. Our six year-old had asked if we could spend it doing things that only six year-olds like to do. I thought we might spend the time doing an activity that would be fun for the whole family. During the course of the discussion, my wife turned to me and not very transparently pleading my son's case, said, "He is only six once. In a few years he'll be off to college and we'll wonder where the time went."

"That's true," I said. "And in a few years we will be seventy and we'll wonder where the time went."

We eventually worked out a compromise that suited everyone. My point is that it is too easy to slip into the parenting role and not come out of it. You are a spouse as well as a parent and maintaining the marital relationship needs work. Make time for each other and don't let months or even years pass before you have a date or a special week-end *alone*.

The arrival of children also means that your relationship is no longer private. Your children observe it, and no matter how hard you try to hide certain aspects of your marriage, your children will be aware of them. Children have limited understanding and are in danger of misinterpreting some of what they see but they are aware of the main currents in your relationship. The implication of this is that you have to be more aware of your own behavior. You also have to go out of your way to explain any significant events in your relationship that affect them. *You also need to reassure them that they are not responsible for your marriage or any of its problems.* If there is a disagreement that is obviously affecting the entire family you need to explain, in simple terms that a child can understand, what is happening, why and how it is going to be resolved. Try not to fight in front of children. It frightens them in the short term, can increase their insecurity in the long-term and generally provides a poor model of conflict resolution. They might also learn some new words that you would rather not be part of their vocabulary.

5. **You have to model love.** It is not just fighting that can provide an inappropriate model for your child - you are a walking, talking symbol of love and marriage. The model you provide them will go a long way in determining their attitudes to marriage in later life. But it's not only your relationship that will determine their chances of a successful union in later life. As you will read, the foundations of the *10 Steps* are built in childhood. The best thing that you can do for your child is to ensure that he or she has the right foundations. If these have not been laid by the age of six or seven, they face a difficult time learning them later.

The core skills of love that need to be learned in childhood include impulse control, respect, sharing, frustration tolerance, self-respect and communication. Of course the young child will not master all the nuances of these difficult areas but they should have developed some of these skills in accordance with their capacity. These skills are communicated via the child's relationship with his or her parents and the model that his or her parent's marriage provides.

Another huge factor that will determine the later success of your child's intimate partnerships is the relationship with the opposite-gender parent. A father is a representative of men in general in the same way that a mother represents all women. The relationship they have with their children will color that child's attitude to that gender for the rest of its life.

In the chapter on attraction, I outlined the dynamics by which parental relationships and the games played between child and parent determine mate attraction and subsequent selection.

One effect of becoming a parent is that it reconnects you with your own childhood. If you had a happy childhood, this can be the cause of great joy, helping you to see the themes in your identity, cherishing family traditions and appreciating your parents anew. If, on the other hand, your childhood was traumatic or difficult, such a reminiscence can have the opposite effect. Dredging up childhood traumas can obviously have an adverse effect on your relationship. Re-experiencing painful events that you have long since buried can throw you into emotional turmoil and impair your child-rearing. This is a time for understanding and nurturing from your partner.

If the adjustment to the arrival of children is a tremendous challenge it is even more so in blended families. This topic is obviously a book in its own right and I will not explore it here. Suffice to say that blended families present all the challenges mentioned in this section with added complications. To begin with, both families start out the relationship from a position of loss. Blending families is part of the resolution of such loss which is why it is so difficult. Enormous changes have to be faced including a change in family values and culture. Child resistance, opposition, splitting and jealousy are not uncommon. If ever a situation called for terrific communication skills, this is it. It is a testimony to people's loving capacity that blended families can work at all and that they can be enormously positive influences on children, who by definition, have experienced significant loss.

Stage 5: Beyond Child-Rearing

When children grow up and leave the home, the focus once again returns to the marriage itself. When this stage is reached, you have probably spent a good twenty years or more raising children and their immediate absence from your home can create as much stress as freedom.

The empty nest is a change and like any change, is stressful. This change also effects your primary relationship. In stage 3, children change the relationship by their very presence, now that they are gone, they change it by their absence. You are left with each other. You can never go back. Frequently, couples in this stage of life have to rediscover their marriage. Your relationship is different than your pre-family relationship for many reasons.

For one thing, unless a concerted effort is made to maintain a peak level of fitness, energy levels decline with age. Energy levels are related to tolerance and positive outlook, so as energy levels decline so does tolerance.[20] As a result we tend to get more "set in our ways" and many older couples are very good at being able to lead separate lives. Concern about declining abilities also leads the ambitious to be more focused on fulfilling their personal goals and dreams and this can often lead an older couple in separate directions. There's nothing wrong with this. I have seen several couples who have continued very successful relationships while spending prolonged time pursuing separate activities.

Retirement poses special problems unless it has been properly planned. It is very important for overall health and performance, to continue to have personal goals. Those people who view their impending retirement as a continuous vacation are typically shocked to

---

[20] There is strong evidence of this relationship between energy and positive outlook. For a good review the reader is referred to the work of professor Robert Thayer who conducted research in this area for thirty years. His book, "The BioPsychology of Mood and Arousal" (Oxford University Press, 1989) is a good outline of his research and theory.

find that they are bored and depressed within a matter of weeks of leaving their job.

Retirement also throws the couple back together for much longer periods than hitherto had been the case. This can create real problems. We promise to be together in sickness and in health but not breakfast, lunch and dinner, too.

The secret to successful retirement and healthy functioning in later years is to pursue "role without responsibility." This allows the senior person to have a role and meaning in their life without the burden of responsibility. The adjustment to a life without children, to the return of the "private" marriage unobserved by offspring, to the vacuum created by retirement, requires planning.

The later years can also be the time when the value of the relationship is really appreciated. As we approach seniority and retirement our drive for material acquisition tends to diminish and we begin to cherish values such as health, family and relationships rather than material possessions. Freed from the rat race, many people who have spent their entire adult life working can finally relax, thus making for a less stressful domestic atmosphere. Consequently, this stage is almost like a different relationship and I know several couples who have experienced their best years when free from both the stresses of daily work and family pressures. These truly can be the golden years, but this will not happen by default. The *10 Steps* still apply but if you have reached this stage of your relationship chances are that you have mastered most, if not all, of them.

Step One

Communicating

Communicating is the first of the *10 Steps* simply because everything else depends on it. Communicating not only entails expressing thoughts and feelings but really <u>understanding</u> your partner. This requires actively listening, suspending judgment and criticism and really making an effort to "walk in your partner's shoes." Understanding how another person feels does not mean that you automatically tolerate and accept their behavior.

Good listening is difficult. It really takes a lot of effort. My clinical work involves listening and one reason I try not to schedule three appointments consecutively, is that after making an effort to listen to for nearly two hours straight, I am really drained. Listening involves quieting your own mind and suspending your own natural inclination to interpret events. A good listener wants to be sure he has heard what the speaker has to say, not what the listener *thinks* he hears or *wants* to hear. Good listening consist of several components.

Good Listening is Judgment Free

The first step in communication is making sure you understand what your partner is saying. All you are trying to do is to transfer your partner's words from his or her mouth to your head. This can be difficult if you have a strong emotional reaction to what is being said. If you disagree with your partner there will be a tendency to start attacking and contradicting before you have even given your partner a chance to express themselves or you a chance to really hear what they have to say. All effective communicators give themselves a chance to understand what is being said to them.

Listening requires your total attention. You cannot listen effectively with one eye on the television or a book or the newspaper. Not only will you not hear correctly you also will not see correctly. Watching someone talking is as important as hearing what they have to say. Non verbal cues can tell you as much about a talker's emotional state as the words they are speaking.

Try listening so that when your partner has finished talking you will be able to accurately reflect back to them what they have just said to you. This is a good practice exercise. The reflection of the communication you have just heard should be judgment free. There will be plenty of time for discussion later.

Listening Practice

Each partner talks uninterrupted for two minutes. When the talker has finished, the listener has to repeat what she or he has just been told without comment.

When you are listening, try not to interrupt, unless you are asking for clarification. Ask for clarification in a non-judgmental way. For example, don't say "You're being hypocritical. You've said you are both angry and happy." Say, "I need some clarification. Could you explain what is making you happy and what is making you angry?"

When your partner has finished talking, you should repeat back to them what you heard them to say. This is critical. Not only will you be sure that you have heard them correctly, it will signal to your partner that they have been heard. If you can do this you have overcome almost half of the communication problem. Many partners complain that their partners don't even hear them. When you really listen to your partner like this, you are validating them. You are not necessarily validating the *content* of what they are saying you are *validating their right to say it.* Even if you do not agree with your partner's comments, they have a right to express them.

All of the above helps create the right communication environment. Listening is not problem-solving. Even if you are bursting to solve what you think your partner's problem is, resist until you have listened to what they have to say.

Creating the right communication environment will promote good interaction. I know a number of people who complain about their partner's poor communication and yet their own behavior actively discourages it.

Early on in my career, I was trying to help a sophisticated, successful London couple manage their communication problems. Joe was a hard driving executive who was good at communicating business objectives and clarifying work goals but less adept at revealing his own emotions. When there was an argument, Joe brooded, saying little until he finally exploded like Krakatoa emerging from the sea. Nicole, an accomplished executive in her own right, refused to be browbeaten this way and headed off to her mother's. Joe's response was not untypical in character from many men; uncomfortable accessing and considering emotions and not very skilled at expressing them.

My task was, therefore, to show them how to communicate within tolerable limits and without Joe exploding and Nicole fleeing. Trying to learn communication skills is often best done in the office of a mental health professional. For one thing, it is someone else's office and not your home which makes it neutral territory, free from associations with past conflicts. For another, the presence of a third party, especially one trained in facilitating communication, injects more restraint into the situation than if the partners were left to their own devices. Indeed, these may be the two biggest reasons for couples to seek help - their problems can be addressed in a way that they cannot do on their own.

Meanwhile, Joe and Nicole were sitting in my office talking about the pattern of communication. Joe admitted that he had difficulty talking about his feelings, especially his anger, and traced the roots of this problem to his mother, a dominant, punitive person. He admitted that he felt embarrassed by some of his emotions and was reticent to express them for fear of being criticized. I invited him to express a feeling - any feeling. After considerable squirming and a lot of hesitation, Joe finally was able to express some anger. Whereupon, Nicole, *rather than appreciating the process of Joe's struggle to express himself,* found fit to criticize the content. Joe stood bolt upright, exclaimed "That's why I never say what I feel!" and promptly stormed off never to be seen again.

Listening, therefore, means giving your partner a fair chance to talk to you. If every time you partner talks about how they feel, you interrupt or criticize, they are not going to be very communicative.

Expressing

Mixing personal thoughts with interpretations of your partner's behavior is one of the biggest communication mistakes. For example, suppose your spouse has just irritated you by committing you to a social event that you did not want to attend. You might be inclined to say something like:

"I am mad. You did that deliberately. You know I did not want to go."

The first part of your statement is undeniable. You are expressing how you feel and no-one can reasonably deny your own feelings. The rest of the utterance, however, is very much deniable, *even if it is true.* You are interpreting your partner's behavior, an activity that all of us abhor. You are telling your partner that you are a mind reader and this will now be the focus of the argument.

The chances are good that your partner will be angry with you for interpreting his or her behavior and will likely come back with something like..

"I did not do it deliberately. You told me that you did not mind going for a short while. Now, you just want to get out of it because you want to watch that TV show instead!"

Of course, he or she has ventured into the interpretation business, too. You can see where this is going - downhill and fast.

Wherever possible, stay with statements about your thoughts and feelings, avoid interpretations and stick with verifiable facts. For example, suppose the above interchange started differently. Suppose you started out with an interpretation-free comment, thus.

"I really don't want to go. Why did you do that?"

This is less inflammatory and gives your spouse a chance to explain his or her actions.

There are clearly times when it is difficult to maintain emotional control and stick to the rules of effective communication. There are many times, however, where these simple basic principles will keep you out of trouble. Practice the basics to improve your communication.

The problem with inadequate communication is that the words that are used and the way they are expressed can lead you completely away from the subject under discussion. Poor communication skills lead to trouble in their own right.

The Power of Words
Words don't just convey meaning, they also carry with them emotional hooks and associations. At some of my seminars I ask the audience to read two lists of words flashed on a screen. The first is a list of words that have negative emotional connotations. This list includes such words as "trauma," "tears," "stress," and "disappointment." Not only do people report feeling stressed when reading these words, you can see it as they are reading the list. Smiles disappear. Faces become tense and taught. Bodies slump. Then they get to read a second, happier list that contains words such as "laughter," "happiness," and "success." The smiles return and muscles relax.

Words are powerful not just because they convey an idea but because they provoke emotional responses. Such power means that words can be used to heal or destroy with equal effect. Two important consequences follow from this.

First, choose your words carefully. As you will see in the chapter on fighting, words can not be taken back. Once you have let them go, they are gone forever and you have to live with the consequences.

Second, listen very carefully to the words that are said to you. Pay special attention to the verbs that people use. As someone who spends a lot of time listening to people, I can tell you that you learn a lot about how someone really feels by listening to their choice of verbs. For example, suppose someone was reporting their reaction to a partner's indiscretion. Different emotions and implications are communicated by each of the following:

"I am amused"
"I am irritated"
"I am surprised"
"I am angered"
"I am destroyed"

The list is endless and the richness of the language allows for a vast array of possibilities all offering subtle nuances of meaning and implied emotion.

The Five Minute Game

Assign fifteen minutes, where you and your partner are alone and undisturbed. Each take five minutes to describe your feelings. Here are some guidelines.

Set the timer for five minutes
Each new idea must begin with the words "I feel…
While your partner is talking, you must remain silent and actively listen
When your partner has finished, repeat what they have said to you.
Do not criticize or interpret their motivation.

Projection

The biggest aspect of communication is projection. Projection, the biggest destroyer of relationships, is the tendency to draw your own conclusions about your partner's motives without ever testing out your version to see whether it is accurate. The reason that listening is so important is that you will actually hear what your partner is saying, rather than imagining what they are saying.

As human beings we are programmed to try to make sense out of the events we observe and experience. This attempt to make meaning comes from our need to order and organize our world, so that we can then control it. All of us write scripts - to use the jargon of *narrative psychology* - that reflect our understanding of the world. Each of our scripts, however, is highly influenced by our own sensitivities and neurotic lens. Two people can witness the same event and have completely different interpretations of it.

> **We don't see reality, we see our version of it.**

Never assume you know another person's viewpoint until you have carefully listened to them.

Communication Inhibitors

There are many people who are reluctant to share their feelings for fear of the response that such open expression might generate. Some are reluctant to be forthcoming because they believe that the listener will be angry, or belittling, or dismissive, or critical or any number of other negative responses. Someone raised in an environment where openly expressed feelings are greeted with hostility will learn to be very careful about what they say. As a result, many people will simply say what it is they think the listener wants to hear. Others, fearing a negative reaction, will say nothing at all. If this is a well practiced communication habit they will soon find it difficult to access, let alone express, true feelings. This can be a very ingrained habit which will take much patience and practice to reverse. The problem can be overcome by creating a safe communication environment, i.e. one without instant criticism.

It is crucial, therefore, to create an environment where partners can speak openly. I had a friend in college who never told his parents anything. They always said they wanted to know, but when he told them anything that was less than positive they would say "Why did you tell us that - we don't want to know." Creating an environment where your partner can be honest is an essential part of communication, especially if they are one of those who have been trained to expect criticism if they express themselves honestly.

Understanding Gender Differences in Communication

There are huge gender differences in communication needs and styles. It is not that one is right or better - they are just different with different strengths in different situations. The simple question, "How was your day?" reveals the differences in gender patterns of communication. A man will give a terse, two line summary of his whole day. A woman will describe in graphic detail the emotional nuances of her encounters. She will primarily describe feelings.

There are three important stages in the communication of emotion.

- The ability to access feelings. Can you feel? What do you feel?

- The ability to process feelings. Do you run? Can you cope?

- The ability to express feelings. Can you express?

How anger is communicated is crucial to the health of a relationship. Is it addressed, processed, dealt with or sublimated into depression, infidelity, passive aggressiveness? Specific techniques for managing anger are discussed on page 163.

How do you express anger?

Do you talk to your partner about it?
Do you talk to anyone about it?
Do you try to bury it?
Do you sulk?
Do you feel sorry for yourself?
Are you frightened by your anger?
Do you feel guilty about your anger?

Accessing Emotions

The experience of emotion is different for men and women. There are physiological differences that mean that, in general, men will not experience emotion as vividly or as easily as women. As a result of different hormones (those chemicals that mediate emotion) men and women don't feel the same way. As a result, the emotional life of a man is not as obvious to him. This frustrates his partner because she, through her enhanced ability to empathize, feels the emotion that she thinks he ought to be experiencing! One of the differences a woman has to accept about her male partner is that he feels in a different way than she does. This does not make him cold, or evil or insensitive.

Of course men do experience emotion, often very intensely. In general they are less able to feel the emotion of another, thus making them seem less sensitive.

Processing Emotions

Until recently, men have not been encouraged to process their emotions. They could busy themselves with single-minded executive tasks essentially distracting themselves from the difficult task of sorting out their complex feelings. Fortunately, there has been a shift in this attitude recently, although it is still tremendous male resistance, for example, to the idea of therapy.

Expressing Emotions

If you are not used to processing and accessing emotions, difficulty expressing them naturally follows. Again this is cultural training that has reinforced the natural male disposition.

Other Forms of Communication

Not all communication is verbal. Everything you do is a form of communication, open to interpretation by one and all. Taking actions that show you understand your partner's viewpoint is a form of good communication. Forgetting your spouse's birthday or your wedding anniversary is poor communication.

Communication requires time and undivided attention. In today's hectic lifestyles that typically means that a couple specifically have to go out of their way to schedule good communication time. It is helpful to get into the habit of scheduling regular communication time. If you do remember to..

- Eliminate all distractions, including children, pets, phones, faxes, etc.

- Don't do it in conjunction with other activities. For example, don't combine communicating with eating. Have your communication time and then go out to dinner.

- Don't do it late at night or when one or other of you is fatigued, sick or completely distracted.

- Communicate in a relaxed setting, where you can sit face-to-face.

Remember, two people will not agree on everything but each partner has the right to express their thoughts and feelings and have them respected. The following story is an example of what happens to people when they stop communicating.

Jane and Todd had enjoyed a stable marriage for fifteen years. Over a period of a few weeks, however, Jane uncharacteristically began to withdraw from intimacy. A few months earlier Jane had lost her part-time job of ten years. At the time, she had been angry with Todd's reaction. He had encouraged her not to look for other work but she wanted some activity outside of the home.

The couple never addressed the situation allowing it to linger on. Todd's interpretation was that Jane's withdrawal was part of her anger towards him. He believed that in time this would pass and, therefore, he did not pursue the discussion. Had Todd discussed the problem he would have found out that his interpretation was wrong. Jane had long since overcome her anger towards him. She was experiencing something different.

The loss of her job had done two things to Jane - it had knocked her confidence and it had landed her back in the home on a full-time basis. As a result, she began grazing and gaining some weight. The extra weight had exacerbated her feelings of lost confidence and lowered her self-esteem. She was ashamed of these feelings and did not want to tell Todd about them. Once they were able to actually address the situation, both of them were relieved and they could go about resolving the problem.

Each couple will develop their own unique communication pattern. Exactly how that pattern manifests itself is less important than the fact that communication happens. Many, many relationships would be almost instantly improved if the partners found a way to talk honestly to each other about their thoughts, hopes and feelings on a regular basis.

Communication is the helium in your marital balloon. Without it you cannot reach very high - in fact, you cannot even take off.

Step Two

Accepting

An intimate relationship is complex. Getting two people with their different desires, habits, attitudes and personalities to fit their lives successfully is like doing a jigsaw puzzle - in the dark. As a relationship evolves, there are fundamental shifts in it which require more adaptation, change and acceptance. The exact details of the challenges that face any one couple will vary, but it is true for all of us that change is inevitable.

Uncertainty

In the 1920's physicists around the world were trying to discover a way of measuring part of an atom called an electron. The best way of measuring this sub-atomic particle was to shine light on it. The problem was that shining light on the electron changed its qualities. The act of measurement changed the phenomena that was being measured. This was the basis of the German physicist Werner Heisenberg's great "uncertainty principle." The principle was enunciated in 1927 and it ultimately led to the Nobel prize for Heisenberg and a breakthrough in theoretical physics.

Relationships are also subject to an uncertainty principle. The more you care for somebody the more you want to spend time with them. The more you spend time with them, the more the relationship changes, especially in its early phases. Even after a long-term relationship has been established there is still uncertainty, no matter how predictable and stable the relationship may appear to be.

A relationship is dynamic. It does not stand still. It is not frozen at the time of your initial attraction. When we are going through difficult times in our relationships we yearn, fruitlessly, for a return to its roots. How many times have you heard yourself, or someone else, say "Why couldn't it be just like it was when we first met?" or "I want the person back that I fell in love with?" Fat chance. You can't go back. If you spend your time looking back over your shoulder at the past you will be stuck on the spot, immobile, calcified as surely as Lot's wife.

A relationship can't be static, you have to keep it moving and that means taking responsibility for your situation and working out constructive ways of progressing. A relationship is like a shark - it needs to keep moving forward to survive. As soon as you accept this and start acting on it, wonderful changes can occur and your relationship can grow. It won't feel the same as the heady days of courtship but it can be just as exciting.

A relationship changes because it has a life of its own and progresses through different stages. Those stages have already been outlined. Over and above these changes inherent in all relationships, however, is the inescapable fact that both partners will change - often quite dramatically - over the course of their union.

One of the most crucial adjustments that any of us have to make in a long-term intimate relationship is acceptance. If you can not practice acceptance you will not be able to maintain a healthy relationship. Acceptance is not about giving in or giving up. Acceptance is about the recognition of certain facts that enable you to manage your relationship effectively.

Here are the eight most important facts that you need to accept to have a chance at a good relationship.

- *You have no control over your partner.*

- *You and your partner will change over time.*

- *Neither of you are perfect.*

- *You always have some responsibility for the state of your relationship.*

- *You and your partner are different.*

The Acceptance Quiz

I slowly adapt to new situations	Never	Sometimes	Often
I question other's views	Never	Sometimes	Often
I am very determined	Never	Sometimes	Often
I seek revenge on those who have been unkind to me	Never	Sometimes	Often
I get agitated waiting	Never	Sometimes	Often
I like to be in control	Never	Sometimes	Often
I don't like change	Never	Sometimes	Often
I find it difficult to let go of my feelings	Never	Sometimes	Often
I can't easily relate to those whose views are different from mine	Never	Sometimes	Often
I dwell on the past	Never	Sometimes	Often

[21]Scoring is given at the bottom of the page

---

[21] Each **Never** answer scores 1 pt, each **Sometimes** answer scores 2pts, each **Often** answer scores 3 pts.
10 pts = The most accepting person I have ever met.
11-15pts= You make a great partner
16-20pts= Good, with a little room for improvement
21-25 pts = Slightly below average level of acceptance, could work to improve it further.
26-30 pts = Oops!! You could get lessons in tolerance from Atila the Hun.

- *You cannot fight over every disagreement.*
- *The excitement of the NEA won't be repeated.*
- *Your relationship is a growing, living entity.*

You Have No Control Over Your Partner

Although you might think you do, in the end any power you have over your mate has been given to you and can, and probably will, be reclaimed. One of the most frustrating aspects of life in general is that we cannot, by and large, control other people. Sometimes, it seems as if we can, but in the end we are generally disappointed that our friends, loved ones and acquaintances don't do what we want them to do. This is no more frustrating than in your partner, with whom you have enmeshed your life and depend on to make decisions and take actions that are in complete accord with your wishes.

Of course, if you have a healthy. balanced relationship, understand each other's strength and weaknesses, communicate effectively and work together as a team, you will have largely resolved this power struggle and have agreed on a workable model of power sharing.

If you are a control freak, however, you will have carefully chosen as your mate somebody that you can control. Indeed, you will have picked somebody that seemed to want your control. Remember, however, that people change and that your control will potentially be a large problem as your relationship develops, as happened in the case described below.

George and Sharon were high school sweethearts. George was two years older than Sharon but when Sharon graduated from high school they got married. George was very domineering, but Sharon did not seem to mind, at least at first. She liked his strength and found security in his determined ways. George appreciated Sharon's willingness to go along with whatever he said, whether that was over minor decisions or major ones. Married at nineteen, Sharon had three children by the time she was twenty-five. As her children began to grow up, Sharon felt she wanted more say in their upbringing and decisions that affected their lives. It was almost as if Sharon could not see why she need to stand up for herself but she did feel the need to stand up for her children.

George did not like Sharon's challenge to, what up to this point, had been his total control. The more she tried to assert herself, the angrier he got. The more he could not control his wife, the more out of control he got. He resorted to physical force on two occasions, which is when I came into the picture.

"I don't understand it," he said, "She's changed. She used to be grateful for me to take charge, now she just wants to do her own thing."

I explained to him that Sharon was never going to stay nineteen forever, that it was inevitable that she would mature and begin to want to make some of her own decisions.

"Well, that's fine,' said George, huffily, "But I just want to go back to the way it was before."

"You can't, " I said. "The cat is out of the bag. Sharon gave you control for nearly ten years and now she is taking it back"

The fact is that once the dynamic had changed and Sharon no longer wanted to give up control of her life, the relationship had changed forever. George could either try to live with it and learn ways of adapting or the relationship was doomed. He made a half-hearted attempt but could never come to terms with the fact that he could no longer have total control and they divorced a year later.

No matter how much control you think you have over your partner, that control is illusory. Sooner or later your partner will wrestle control back from you, whether you like it or not, which you won't. Almost all adults resent being controlled by other people. It's only a matter of time before they assert themselves.

Which brings us to the next important fact that you need to accept.

You And Your Partner Will Change Over Time.

Although your partner's fundamental personality structure will probably not change, many other aspects will. Experience will create changes in maturity that might change personality characteristics especially after the age of forty. The human body changes over time in many ways and this can lead to not just physical but emotional and psychological changes. Life events, some predictable and some completely unforeseen, will provide many challenges to your partner with unknown effects.

An old adage directed specifically to those embarking on a relationship is "don't expect your partner to change." Generally, this is good advice. If you enter a relationship expecting a partner to change some trait or behavior, you are likely to be disappointed. It is not that change won't happen. Change is inevitable. It's just that the changes that occur are not what you expect or necessarily want.

I once got a phonecall from a young man who was about to get married. He said he did not feel the need to consult with me in person, he just wanted to ask me one question over the phone. This sort of telephone consultation is not my normal practice but I was intrigued and asked him what his question was. He explained that he was planning to get married but that his fiancee had an annoying habit (according to him) of "impulsive spending". He had talked to her about this behavior and she had promised that she would change but had not thus far. He wanted me to confirm that she would indeed be able to stop doing this once they were married. A million thoughts went through mind. How impulsive was his fiancée? Did she have a full blown clinical condition or was this an isolated behavior? Had she really promised to change? Did *she* see anything unusual in her behavior? *Was* there anything unusual in her behavior?

I explained that I was not normally in the habit of giving advice over the phone without much more information. I would, of course, be pleased to see them both to assess and advise them on the situation.

"No. it's really not that important," said the man.

"I think that calling a mental health professional to ask whether your future wife can change a behavior that's obviously causing you some annoyance is more important than you are making out," I suggested.

This did not shift him from his position of wanting a brief reply and I decided to give him one. So, after expressing all my caveats for making an uninformed opinion, I said the following.

"I don't think you fiancee is going to change - or at least the way you want it to. I think her behavior is going to get worse. But even if she does change this behavior, your question is really about your ability to accept uncertainty. I know one thing for sure, that in the course of marriage your wife will change in many ways. If you cannot tolerate that thought you might want to reconsider marriage."

This clearly was not the answer he was looking for. He told me I was wrong and I never heard from him again.

During the course of a relationship, especially marriage, the following changes occur.

First, you and your partner will age physically. Such changes can have an enormous effect on your attitude and behavior. Changes in energy levels, sex drive, physical and even mental abilities are all part of the aging process. As we get older, our bodies change shape, we have a tendency to gain weight, our immune system efficiency declines and we are more likely to develop conditions that affect our lifestyle.

> **Middle age - the point at which you start paying for the excesses of your lifestyle rather than enjoying them.**

You and your partner will change emotionally. There are various developmental stages of emotional development. Physical adolescence ends in the late teens or early twenties but in many ways adolescence does not end for most people until they are thirty-five. For some people, adolescence never ends. The twenties and early thirties are an age when most people are basking in the delights and trauma of their own independence. As they are finding their way in the world, they are discovering themselves, learning about their personalities, their strengths and weaknesses. In the more enlightened members of the species this process continues throughout life, but its effects are most dramatic in the twenties and thirties.

As we mature, we change our interests, attitudes, and behavior. This is generally a good thing - but it can create difficulties for our partners who have a vested interest in keeping the status quo, whose own neuroses or sensitivities require that their partners not change at all. This is one of the major puzzles facing the couple about to embark on a long-term relationship - no-one knows what the long term will bring. Accepting this fact, and agreeing to make a commitment despite the uncertainty, are fundamental to a successful union.

The developmental stages of a relationship were outlined in the last chapter. If you have a family, the arrival of children will signal changes in your priorities, financial needs, emotions and every other aspect of your life. When the children have developed independent lives you are faced with another completely different situation.

During the course of your marriage there will be events and stresses that neither of you have had to face before. You and your partner's reaction to these events are unknown until they happen.

Your partner will change in the course of the relationship

And because you too, are a partner, this means that you will change over time, too.

Neither Of You Are Perfect
Both of you are human and will make mistakes. Forgiving yourself as well as your partner when this happens will be critical to the success of your union. If you can't practice forgiveness, you will be constantly stuck in the past.

All of us make mistakes. All of us take actions that, intentionally or otherwise, hurt our partners. That is part of being human and there is no escape from it. Obviously, premeditated, deliberately hurtful actions are abusive. Unfortunately, under the wrong conditions, most people who are loving, kind individuals can lash out and say and do things that are harmful to their loved ones.

Intimate relationships generate powerful emotions because not only are the partners invested in each other's lives they also know each other so well that they know which buttons to push when there is a confrontation. As you will see in the section on learning how to fight (Step 6), you cannot take back words once you have said them, or retrace actions once you have done them. We all say and do things that we wish we could take back. The best you can do in that situation is to apologize and ask for forgiveness.

Many couples cannot forgive. It is amazing to me that people who barely seem to remember what the day of week it is, can recall with vivid clarity, a supposed slight that happened to them so long ago there is some question as to whether it even happened in the same geological period. Of course, once one partner starts reviving ancient history the tendency is for the other to start reaching into the outer limits of their memory banks for their historical hurts.

Such acrimonious history lessons are generally a sign of a relationship in trouble. It is not that wounding comments or hurtful actions should be dismissed as trivial, clearly they are not. It's just not helpful to continuously use these as weapons against each other. For one thing, continually rehashing old sores simply keeps them alive and can only escalate tension and make conflict more likely. For another, recalling ancient history in an emotional, confrontational way means that that you have not resolved the underlying conflict and are hanging on to the hurt.

Hanging on to the hurt is not helpful for either of the partners or the relationship. The person carrying around the hurt is the one who is most affected by it. So letting go of the hurt is most helpful to the person carrying it. As you will see in Step 9, forgiveness is more beneficial to the person doing the forgiving.

You Always Have Some Responsibility For The State Of Your Relationship

No matter how much you might want to blame your partner, you always have a role in, and some responsibility for, the events in your relationship. Your may not have the lion's share of the responsibility but you always have some.

Social commentators and experts depict a crisis in our society - a crisis of responsibility. It seems fashionable for people not to own up to the consequences of their actions. The victim mentality surfaces everywhere. A burglar is injured robbing a house and sues his victims. A sports star feels his contract has been preempted by a bigger signing and demands a re-negotiation. People do all manner of silly and dangerous things and when they have negative consequences they search the fine print of life for somebody else to blame. Is this really a contemporary problem or is this just human nature?

It is a feature of human nature to defend the ego and present oneself in a positive light. So at one level this is basic human characteristic, one frequently demonstrated by six year-olds. A schoolteacher friend of mine recounts how she saw one of her first grade charges punch a classmate. When suitably reproached about his behavior the child honestly replied, "I didn't do it. My right hand moved on its own." So, I am sure that the evasion of responsibility is a hallmark of the human mind. There are, however, several factors in contemporary society that exacerbate this natural tendency.

First, there is a fundamental confusion over the <u>difference between tolerating and understanding</u>. The attitude has developed that if a behavior can be explained it is acceptable. Freud is often blamed for this confusion because the development of psychoanalysis shed light on motivation and led to a greater understanding of why people act the way they do. To blame Freud is in many ways unfair. Any predominant model of motivation whether it is psychoanalytic, behavioral, social or medical will run into the same problem. When motivation can be explained, we make the logical error of absolving the person of responsibility.

Since the middle of this century there has been a shift in the predominant model of explanation away from the psychological to the biological. Now motivation is explained (and very often misunderstood) as a biological phenomena. This person ran amok with a submachine gun because he is sensitive to food chemicals, that person did not know what she was doing because the chemicals in her brain were out of whack.

Medical explanations seem to have authority and a consistent logic but even though they explain behavior they, too, don't absolve the responsibility for action (except in the case of a person who permanently cannot assess or control their actions, e.g. the severely mentally handicapped or retarded).

Consider the food chemicals/submachine gun scenario described above. If somebody knew they were allergic to food chemicals, it is their responsibility to manage the problem. A responsible person would check labels, learn to identify potentially toxic foods and generally take great care not to expose themselves to harmful toxins. If they did not know about the problem, they still have to manage the onset of unusual violent symptoms.

It should be noted that the relationship between biological events and behavior is nowhere near as precise or as specific as we are lead to believe. Many people exposed to the same critical biological and environmental factors, respond differently.

Behavior is enormously complex and the underlying biology is only one factor influencing it. It is simplistic in the extreme to associate one biological event to a specific action. Yet this precisely what we do, and based on this simplistic view, we absolve responsibility. As our world gets more sophisticated about both biology and psychology and as we comprehend more about human motivation, the confusion between understanding and tolerating will grow.

To demonstrate that understanding is not the same as tolerating, consider the following. We know a lot about what makes psychopaths tick; a cold, hostile upbringing, poor attachment and the absence of conscience. History's most evil demons suffered from such a background. Such understanding hardly allows us, however, to tolerate the concentration camps of eastern Europe, the stalags of Siberia or the killing fields of Cambodia. Understanding is a wonderful thing. It can lead to compassion and confusion, and often leads to both.

This confusion between tolerating and understanding is reflected in attitudes towards responsibility within the relationship.

One couple was typical of many when they recently sought help. In the first few minutes it was quickly established that the man suffered from depression. The depression, he claimed, prevented him from feeling certain emotions (e.g he was rarely upbeat) and doing certain actions (e.g spending quality time with his children) within the marriage. His wife said that she understood the nature of his problem and although it made life more difficult for her (she has to entertain the children single-handedly, put up with her husband's constant irascibility) she tolerated this state of affairs while at the same time being very frustrated and angry. He claimed he wished he could do more, but does not.

As I watch this dialogue unfold, two of the burning questions in my mind are:

"Is he using these symptoms to get out of his responsibilities?"

"Is she allowing him to absolve himself from responsibility, and if so, why?"

An analysis of his depression showed that there was no strong family history of the complaint and that it began shortly after the birth of their second child. Further analysis of his past shows that he was an only child (yes, you can see where this is going, can't you?). Moreover, the couple admit that the second child was something of a mistake, more wanted by the wife. His depression is really unexpressed anger about the second child. She realized this and considered it a trade-off for having her second child. He pouts, she puts up with it and they both call it depression so they can avoid the real issue.

Who has responsibility for the state of this relationship? Clearly they both do.

> **Both partners *always* have some responsibility for the state of the relationship**

The vast majority of people who come for couples counseling sit on my couch thinking, if not explicitly stating, "All you need to do is fix my partner and our relationship will be okay." My first goal in this situation is to get each part to accept they have some responsibility, no matter how unfairly their partners may have treated them.

A man once admitted to me his multiple affairs - he seemed addicted to the extra-marital relationship. He boasted that he once had four affairs simultaneously - a tremendous feat of time management and organizational prowess if not moral fortitude. His wife was equally talented at ignoring all the obvious signs of her husband's infidelity and did her best impression of an ostrich when the subject was raised. Neither party's behavior excused or exonerated the other's: they simply both had some responsibility for the state of the relationship.

Getting one partner or another to agree to the responsibility is not only the first step in my counseling, it is also the hardest. But there is no point progressing any further with therapy unless this is agreed by both parties. Once it is agreed, real change is possible. To paraphrase John F. Kennedy's remarks:

Ask not what my marriage can do for me, but what I can do for my marriage.

You And Your Partner Are Different

There are likely to be big individual differences between you and your partner as a result of gender, personality and culture. Typically, the bigger the differences, the more difficult the relationship. This is why couples of similar socio-economic backgrounds fare better than those who are not, all other things being equal. Evidence shows that religious similarity is a big factor in marital stability.[22] People with the same religious backgrounds are more likely to share the same core values than those who do not have similar religions. Whatever the nature of these differences, and there will be many even in the best relationships, they need to be addressed and accommodated. Rather than moan about these differences, successful couples learn how to harness them and use them effectively.

Your partner will not think the same way as you, neither will they do everything the same way you do.

It is unhealthy for one partner to take on all the tasks involved in running a joint venture like a relationship. You need to accept that your partner will do things differently from the way you do. Get over it! You have to learn to delegate.

Child rearing practices of recent generations are one reason why responsibility is often shirked. In recent generations, self-discipline has not been a fundamental tenet of parenting. The "feel-good" movement aimed at maintaining a child's self-esteem at its highest point, no matter what, has led to self-indulgence and an inability to tolerate frustration. In a society geared to convenience and speed and where attention span can be measured in milliseconds, there is no experience of gratification delay.

Watch people waiting in line at the bank or the supermarket. Most of them positively bristle with tension if they have to wait more than a few moments. If, by some horrible chance there is a further delay, some become positively enraged. It's no wonder that most businesses spend a lot of effort and money to ensure their customers do not have to endure waiting.

The need to compromise should be obvious to most who have tried their hand at a meaningful intimate relationship. But if people

---

[22] Lehrer EL, Chiswick CU., Religion as a determinant of marital stability. Demography 1993 Aug;30(3):385-404

can't tolerate the minor inconvenience of a five minute wait in the checkout line of the supermarket, how are they going to cope when their partner wants a totally different type of vacation, has different ideas about the size of the family or does not want to have sex? How is someone who is used to getting their own way going to cope when they discover their partner thinks and acts differently and has different wants and needs?

There are big differences between you and your mate. These differences do affect everyday functioning. Different ways of doing small things can get really aggravating if they are constantly repeated. She drives cautiously, he drives aggressively. She likes it warm, he likes it cold. She cooks it one way, he cooks it another. She puts the toilet seat down , he puts it up. He snores, she doesn't.

Accepting the differences and finding ways of working together, or at least minimizing the frustration with each other is key. In mature relationships, the different strengths of each partner are recognized and utilized in the right situation. Recently, the wife of a couple I was counseling, complained bitterly about the fact that she perceived herself as more "giving" in the relationship than her husband. As the three of us discussed this situation, it became clear that overall she felt her husband contributed as much to the relationship as she did and that they were equally committed to each other. She just felt an inbalance in their giving.

I asked her a tough question. "Why do you assume that you are both going to be equals in everything? Why do you assume that you are both going to have equal patience, equal flexibility and equal tolerance?"

The question was rhetorical. It is unreasonable to expect couples to be equally matched on very attribute. As long as overall there is a fair distribution of characteristics, a relationship can work. A relationship will not work too well if there is a lop-sided distribution of important characteristics or if one partner is totally inflexible on an important issue (e.g. commitment). Each partner will have different strengths and weaknesses. Unfortunately many people assume that there is a sort of automatic natural justice that dictates that all partners will have equal strengths. Many get disappointed when they find out that this is not the case.

> **A relationship needs *balance* not complete equality in everything**

Many of these differences can be traced to gender differences. The example mentioned above was a classic case of gender differences. To the wife, 'giving' meant being sensitive to the partner's needs and responding quickly to them. Women are simply better at this than men. On one occasion, a wife was complaining about her husband's lack of sensitivity and a litany of other deficiencies, the root of which was that he was not like her. He was not like her because he was a man. "Madam," I said in all sincerity, "I think you would have been better off marrying a woman."[23]

Delegation is an important relationship skill. You need to accept that there are certain tasks and activities that your partner should have control over. This means that you have given up control - if not your influence.[24] Accepting the need to concede control and responsibility on some issues is difficult but does happen in the effective relationship.

One of the biggest reasons for divorce is that many people are so selfish that they can't even consider compromise. In today's world, where there is an obsession with the outcome rather than the process, the bottom-line rather than the product, the criteria all too often is "what's in it for me." Instead of a me-too mentality you need a we-two outlook. The team, the relationship, needs to be the higher focus.

---

[23] I have made a similar argument to many a man complaining that his wife was not like him.
[24] In a corporate setting delegation does not necessarily imply giving up control. The manager doing the delegating has the ultimate control and responsibility which he keeps by setting limits, getting feedback and monitoring. I am using the term delegation in the domestic setting to mean actually giving control and responsibility over to your partner on some projects. They will likewise do the same for you.

If you think that the relationship exists to merely serve your needs, you are in for a rude awakening. Even those who have partners willing to be subservient will, in the end, discover that a one-sided relationship doesn't work.

If you are not prepared to accept compromise, don't bother with an intimate relationship.

Individuality

Where does individuality fit into the context of the we-two relationship? Sometimes the we-two relationship is riddled with dependency. The partners have an unhealthy dependence on each other and, as we shall later, dependence is not love.

One of the values of a secure attachment is that it provides partners with confidence and security. With that confidence and security they, as individuals, can go out into their world and go about the business of achieving their potential. A secure relationship should provide, therefore, the basis for greater self-improvement and actualization. All too often, I see relationships where individuality is stifled because of possessiveness, jealousy or the mistaken assumption that couples should only indulge in joint activities.

One person cannot completely fulfill another person's needs. No matter how loving, talented or skilled, no one person can meet all the needs of their partner. What they can do, however, is to allow the other person the freedom to find their own individuality. As you will read in Step 7, this can be done by giving time, encouragement and support and by providing a stable, secure and loving relationship.

<u>You Cannot Fight Over Every Disagreement</u>

You have to choose your battles carefully. No matter how good a relationship is, two people will not agree on everything. If you fight over every difference, your relationship will be a war zone that nobody wants to inhabit. If you cannot delegate and compromise you will be spend a lot of your time, frustrated and angry.

Learning to let go of the emotion generated by petty annoyances is important for you and your relationship's survival. Step

6, provides the rules for fighting fair with some tips on how to minimize frustration. There will be times when petty annoyances become the focus for major issues. Many years ago I saw a tabloid headline that read "WIFE KILLS HUSBAND FOR NOT PASSING THE SALT." You don't have to be a psychologist to realize that there was more to this homicide than table etiquette.

The issue of compromise is particularly relevant in the early stages of living together when you are learning about each other's daily habits. This is especially true in your first experience of living with someone else. When you embark on a relationship for the first time, you are coming either from the family home or from a period of being single and being able to do what you wanted, when you wanted. It has not occurred to you that there are other ways of doing things, or worse still, you might have to put up with them.

There is always danger of "crying wolf" if you argue over every minor annoyance. It might be difficult for your partner to know how important an issue is to you if you make a big fuss over every little detail.

The Novel Erotic Attachment Won't Be Repeated
Hopefully, your relationship will still constitute an erotic attachment - but novelty cannot be recaptured. It is novelty that gives the NEA that special excitement, and that has to fade once you get to know your partner. This does not mean to say that sex in particular and life in general can't be fun, or even better, as your partnership progresses but you will not maintain the initial excitement.

In Step 8, there are suggestions and advice on how to keep romance alive. It is important to accept, however, that the heady days of courtship are gone. If you are hooked on this stage of a relationship you are in for a disappointment. If you really are an NEA addict, get a good lawyer and a large bank account. Multiple relationships are expensive.

Your Relationship Is Constantly Evolving

You cannot take your relationship or you partner for granted - both are constantly evolving as are you. You never know whether around the next corner you are going to be run over by the Family Publishers Clearinghouse Team anxious to deliver your $10,000,000 prize or an Family Publishers Clearinghouse Truck anxious to deliver periodicals to your neighborhood stores. Sometimes Horribly Inconvenient Things Happens.

You have already read about the different developmental stages of a relationship and the special challenges that they present. Many of these challenges will be completely new to you. During your relationship you will face many events for the first time. Sometimes these events are conveniently spaced so that you rarely get overwhelmed. Other people, however, have the misfortune of being buried under an avalanche of troubles. One woman I knew lost her father and brother in separate incidents, had a son undergo major brain surgery, was robbed and lost her job all within a matter of three weeks!

We are shaped by the events that we have to experience and as a result, relationships change as the partners change.

The Four Stages of Acceptance

From studies on grieving, it is widely accepted that acceptance of loss consists of four different stages. Although this work is derived mainly from work done with those who have lost a loved one, the psychological phenomena is applicable to loss in general.

A relationship can and does put constraints on behavior, especially if the person has not come straight from another relationship and has therefore lived on their own prior to this attachment.

In a relationship you go from an "I" orientation to a "We" orientation and, as a result, there is a certain loss of freedom, independence and control. Those are always issues in a relationship but more pronounced in the early stages where the transition from I to We is more traumatic. As the relationship progresses there may be a loss of dreams, aspirations and opportunities. There is no question that relationships involves costs; a good relationship more than amply compensates for these costs.

It is necessary to come to terms with these costs, otherwise they will turn into resentments and create more problems.

The one advantage of losses in a relationship (as compared to deaths) is that you have a choice. Relationship engendered losses are endured as part of your conscious decision to participate in the relationship. As a result, you still have some control which makes the loss more tolerable.

Accepting the concession of something important, like total freedom, control or independence, is going to be much easier if you can see what you have gained in return. Sometimes it is too easy to see the negative aspects of what you have lost rather then the positive aspects of what you have gained.

It is important to focus on the benefits of a relationship. It's all too easy to take them for granted. Some obvious gains are listed in the box below. Can you think of others that are applicable to you?

Relationship Gains
What benefits are there for you in the relationship?

Companionship
Friendship
Intimacy/Sex
Emotional Security
Financial Security
Care-taking
Opportunities
Dreams and Goals
Family

The human tendency to seek novelty has already been highlighted and this often leads to an overly positive view of how green the next pasture really is. To fully understand the nature of the relationship that you have you must consider what the alternative would really be like. Far too many people overvalue their alternatives and this is damaging to their appreciation of what they already have.

Appraising Your Relationship

What would it be like if you no longer had the relationship? Ask the following questions. Distinguish between the benefits of a particular relationship and from relationships in general.

Where would I be living?
What would my financial status be?
What would happen to my social life?
Where would I get my emotional needs met?
Would my physical needs be met?
What would my lifestyle be like?
What about other family members?
What about dreams and opportunities?

Denial

The first step in dealing with loss is often to deny it. In the early stages of mourning there is disbelief that a loved one has died and a sense that they are going to appear at any moment. Some relationship costs, like moving further away from family, cannot be denied as a fact but their significance can be minimized. For example, a young couple consulted me for their relationship difficulties having moved to the area a year earlier. One of the biggest problems was that the young woman had moved away from her family. Although she realized that she missed her family she had not appreciated that the increased distance was the predominant cause of her depression. Neither had she realized that the anger directed towards her husband because of his insistence on their relocation, was undermining the relationship.

Denial of relationship incurred losses increases the risk of anxiety and depression and will have a negative impact on the relationship. There may be vague feelings of dissatisfaction and anger and these may be focused on other issues. For example, the young woman mentioned above initially complained about her husband's lack of drive not his insistence on relocation.

Typical relationship costs

Loss of friends
Loss of some freedom
Further away from friends and family
Change of jobs
Moving to different location
Loss of some control

Anger

Anger is experienced on the perception that you have been treated unfairly. If you believe that you have experienced a loss because of your partner's actions you are going to be mad with them. In this case, before you do anything drastic, you need to subject your thoughts to a reality check.

Sometimes, you have been unfairly treated and the responsibility for the cost lies squarely at the feet of your partner. If you partner has squandered money without your knowledge or been unfaithful, then you have every right to be angry. Sometimes, it is less clear cut. The young woman in the relocation example above, agreed to relocate with her husband. She could have refused to move, or voice more opposition. She soon recognized that her anger was partly at herself for not realizing how difficult the relocation would be.

Some anger is inappropriate because it is based on unrealistic expectations. For example, a man consulted with me complaining about his fiancee. She just would not wait on him, hand and foot. He had a heretofore unchallenged, sexist view of marriage. That someone would violate this perception seemed totally unfair to him!

Sadness

It is appropriate to be sad when you experience loss. Self-pity is a natural part of sadness and only becomes a problem if it is prolonged. Sadness is not depression. Depression is primarily a loss of energy, which often accompanies sadness but they are not the same.

Acceptance

Acceptance is much easier when you can see the gains that result from the sacrifices that you are making. Acceptance is easier when you can find positive meaning in the act of accepting .

Accepting is not the same as being negative. Do not accept with resignation. Accept because by so doing, you get an improved relationship in return.

If you cannot accept the above truths, expect a lonely time in your relationship. You cannot control everything, or another person. That expectation is doomed to disappointment and disillusionment.

If you are unable to accept and compromise, your relationships will be difficult, if you have any relationships. I have literally dozens of stories about couples who made their relationships work by giving up some goals so they could realize others. Giving up personal goals and dreams is by no means necessary. Many good relationships enhance the possibility of meeting lifelong ambitions. Sometimes, however, those personal goals have to go for the sake of developing the relationship. Giving up an ambition is hard - it often feels like amputation. Sometimes, however, that sacrifice itself empowers the relationship, as it did in the following case.

John and Sherry were an outgoing couple. Living on the edge of a large metropolitan area with two daughters, a dog and a comfortable lifestyle. Like all couples they had their fair share of disagreements but one sensed that theirs was a stable, loving relationship. Both partners were devoted parents and they loved nothing more than spending weekends as a family engaged in outdoor activities: camping, horse riding and a variety of competitive sports that their young daughters, in their middle childhood, were just experiencing.

John ran his own small business and Sherry freelanced some graphic design work. John would help out with child care to allow Sherry some time for her freelance work and so it was that one Spring Friday evening, John and his daughters were preparing a surprise dinner, a homemade pizza, for Sherry who was off in town delivering some work.

I don't know how you react when a family member is late but John and his daughters were so engrossed in the preparation of their surprise dinner that they didn't even notice that the woman of the household was thirty minutes late. When Sherry had not turned up an hour after her expected arrival time, however, John did get a little concerned, although he tried not to communicate this to his children.

By the time the police came to the door, the pizza was cold and uneaten. There had been an accident. A slick road, an inattentive driver, fateful timing and Sherry was in the intensive care unit in a coma.

What happened in the days and weeks in the hospital immediately after the accident must have influenced subsequent events. When John arrived at the Intensive care unit, he was told that Sherry's life hung in the balance. The lower part of her body had been crushed and she had sustained head injuries. She was bleeding internally, and her lungs and kidneys were failing.

If you have ever sat in a hospital waiting the medical fate of a loved one you might have some idea of what John experienced that night and for the following forty-eight hours. John's whole experience of the world completely changed. Time stood still. Every sound seem magnified. Thoughts oscillated wildly from making funeral arrangements on the one hand to planning a recuperation vacation on the other. Through the heightened perception that descends like an electric storm when death lurks, John found himself constantly pinching himself, trying to convince the greater part of his mind that this was a terrible nightmare. A thousand times that night, in the agonizing battle between denial and reality, John found himself trying to pretend that Sherry was going to be just fine. A thousand times reality shrieked back the undeniable facts.

Sherry survived the night. And the next night, too. Gradually she pulled back from the precipice of death, helped substantially by modern medicine but mostly by the love and devotion of her family. Internal injuries were stabilized. Her head injuries were not as severe as was first feared. Her speech returned. Her spirits revived. Her legs didn't. No amount of physical therapy was going to make a difference. She would be confined to a wheel chair for the rest of her life.

I am not sure any of us know how we would cope with being a vibrant, outgoing, thirty-seven year-old wife and mother of two daughters, literally cut down in our prime. No more simple activities that we take for granted like walking, standing, driving. For Sherry, no more horse riding, a life bereft of easy mobility, a life where every move has to planned with all the thoughtfulness of a competition chess match.

This devastating event changed the lives of all of them. For John, life now meant ensuring Sherry's mobility. More child care demands. A complete change in how his own needs both mental and physical would be met.

The four stages of reaching acceptance have been described above. Denial could only be short-lived and lasted only a few hours on that first night vigil in the hospital. Sadness soon followed. Depression is not sadness - it is a loss of energy that comes from the feeling of helplessness. Everyone in that family felt the crushing helplessness of the situation. They felt it until they had a plan, reconnected with hope and had a vision of a future that was possible.

Sherry took the lead. She would not allow anger keep her trapped in helplessness. She rallied her family and basically told then that she could cope if they could. She could help them if they helped her. There was to be no recrimination or bitterness. They had their lives to lead and they would do the best they could. They had each other. Or did they?

Situations like this can make or break a family. John could have decided that life with a wife in a wheel chair was too much to bear. He would not have been the first to walk out of a tragic situation. He could have decided that leaving was impossible, the guilt would have been too great, but stayed on in a half-committed way out of obligation rather than love. Had he done so he would have trapped Sherry and his two daughters in a web of helplessness and despair. But John did neither of these things. He committed himself more than ever.

The courageous acceptance of this tragedy by both John and Sherry enabled them to grow as individuals, as a couple and as a family. They define commitment.

Life is full of events that you never wanted to face.

Circumstances happen that are completely beyond your control and you are put into situations that have no wonderful solutions. These situations make you deal with the unthinkable. If you refuse to accept them you stay stuck with the unthinkable - if you accept them, they become manageable. I should know.

When my first son was born, I was the proudest father around. Here was a beautiful baby and I had all the wonderful things he was going to do in life, all worked out. I envisioned him as a great sportsman, academic, businessman, husband and son. I was going to have so much fun showing him the world. We would travel together, play together, pray together.

As a baby Josh had difficulty sleeping. I would walk around the dining room table with him on my shoulder for what seemed like hours getting him off to sleep. As soon as I put him down he would wake up and we resumed our march. His sleeplessness and my fitness were thus positively correlated. By the time he was a toddler he seemed very alert and advanced and seemed to have a grasp of sophisticated concepts.

We proudly enrolled him in pre-school fully expecting him to flourish and shine. Things did not quite work out that way. After a few weeks, the teacher called to say she wanted to talk to us in private. Josh was bright - he just was not mixing in with the other kids. He was aloof. I knew some of the possibilities but I did not want to contemplate them. Perhaps he just needed a little more time.

A year passed. Josh could speak words but couldn't really hold a conversation. He was a good child - too good. All our friends envied how quiet and placid he was but little did they know.

We re-enrolled him for the next year in the Montessori school. He continued to be socially unresponsive. He could speak a few words, was not disruptive and seemed to be attached to us. But he also had stereotyped hand-flapping and chin banging movements. By the time we consulted a specialist I did not really need her to tell me the diagnosis. I knew my son was autistic.

Autism[25] is a difficult diagnosis for a parent to accept. For the most part, the children are good-looking and at first glance seem normal. They have periods where they function almost normally but can rapidly swing to social unresponsiveness and horrendous tantrums that suggest total terror and complete sensory overload. One time, I had taken Josh to a carnival. The noise - it could have been the music, the ambient noise of the crowds or some noise I never even heard - freaked him out. I tried to talk to him, comfort him and even remove him from the situation - all to no avail. I am standing in this place with an inconsolable, terrified child drawing attention from everyone within two hundred yards. I am frustrated, angry, helpless, desolate. I want to shake him, gag him, love him, cure him. I know that in twenty minutes he will calm down.

Another time, we had taken him to a big toy store at Christmas time. As the other children excitedly explored the festively stocked shelves and ran frenetically from section to section, Josh sat stationary

---

[25] Like many psychiatric diagnoses, autism really describes a family of disorders that share similar characteristics. The defining symptoms of autism are social unresponsiveness, impaired language especially expressive language, stereotyped hand movements, heightened sensory awareness, high anxiety and poor social skills. Autistic children seem as if they are "in their own world" and are often unreachable. The condition is almost certainly a biochemical abnormality that interferes with neurotransmission.

in the middle of an aisle staring into space. My wife, Josh's stepmother, wept openly.

For a long time, one of my ambitions was to have a conversation with my son that consisted of more than just him echoing back what I had said, or regurgitating some obscure association that was beyond my comprehension. I wanted him to play ball and ride a bike. Most of all, I wanted him to see the world that I knew.

I don't know how much I have accepted Josh's fate. I know that our worlds only occasionally intersect. Fortunately, Josh is a high functioning autistic and now that he is older we have had the semblance of real conversations and meaningful contact. I certainly have accepted that Josh has deficits and that his world is quite different than mine. Now, rather than being distressed by this fact, I relish it. I know that wherever we go he will provide a perspective that I simply would never have appreciated. A couple of years ago, I took him to Atlanta to watch a ballgame. He seems to like baseball but I was not sure what he would find interesting. It turned out that the big centerfield scoreboard was what caught his imagination. It was not the scores or the information that entranced him, but the scoreboard structure itself, the flashing lights and the birds dancing and sitting on top of it. He could have watched it for hours.

I wish that there were no such thing as autism and I hope you are never faced with its challenges. I have suffered the pain and despair of the diagnosis. But although I did not want to take this turn in the road, I have gained much from it. Josh is a beautiful child and I love him dearly. He has taught me a lot about patience, tolerance, gratitude, perspective, love, but most of all, myself. I wanted to teach him about the world and yet this child, who can barely communicate and lives at a tangent to my world, has ended up teaching me.

I do not know what the future holds for Josh. There is progress and hope. Whatever will be, will be. That's just the way it is.

Step Three

Committing

A relationship requires commitment to make it work. A relationship without commitment isn't a relationship - it's a loose arrangement. Commitment is the glue that keeps a relationship together. Most people think of commitment merely in terms of sexual fidelity but real commitment goes far beyond the promise of sexual loyalty. You can be totally faithful to your partner but still not be committed to the relationship.

Commitment involves the consideration of the relationship in all matters. It is a commitment to consider how any action you might take, affects your partner and the relationship. This does not mean that you will always make personal decisions secondary to your relationship. It does mean, however, that you make every effort to consider the impact of your actions and treat the relationship and your partner with fairness, respect and without harm. Various studies have shown commitment to be a predictor of long-term marital happiness and stability.[26]

Lack of commitment creates insecurity which erodes the relationship. Moreover, commitment is essential if you are going to successfully tackle the problems that inevitably arise in a relationship. Lack of commitment will prevent the hard work required to implement the *10 Steps* and truly love. This is why it is not possible to be completely committed to two people at the same time. Conflicts

---

[26] For example, in a paper in the International Journal on Aging and Human Development (1990;31(3):189-195) entitled, "The long-term marriage: perceptions of stability and satisfaction.," Lauer RH, Lauer JC, and Kerr ST found that "being married to someone they liked as a person and enjoyed being with; <u>commitment to the spouse and to marriage (</u>my underline); a sense of humor; and consensus on various matters such as aims and goals in life, friends, and decision making," were predictors of happiness and stability in 100 couples who had been married for forty-five years or more.

obviously arise which put limits on your commitment and a limited commitment is no commitment at all.

The emotional effects of having multiple partners limit commitment in many ways. Multiple partners create stress and divide time and attention, especially if these extra relationships are clandestine. More significantly, multiple relationships remove the motivation to make a relationship work. Let us suppose that you were having an argument with partner A. If you had multiple commitments it would be easy to minimize partner A by reassuring yourself that you don't have these problems with partner B. Having a relationship with partner B makes it unlikely that you will do the hard work of working on your relationship with partner A. As a result, multiple relationships remove commitment and the motivation to resolve issues.

One of the strengths of a monogamous relationship is that it does indeed provide the motivation to work at resolving problems. Often, however, a partner will look outside the relationship when there are dilemmas and problems to be solved. When a partner has an affair, commitment is naturally violated. An affair, therefore, is a hostile act. It is a hostile act that is always damaging and often life-threatening to the relationship.

A relationship can not, therefore, survive other intimate commitments. Many times in counseling, I have seen distressed couples come for counseling with one party completely indifferent and aloof. It is then that I know, maybe even before their partner has sensed it, that they are involved with someone else. Sure enough, after a few minutes, or a session or two, rarely more, the partner having the extramarital affair will announce that the current relationship is irreconcilable and want a divorce.

> **It is not possible to reconcile differences in one relationship while one party is romantically involved with someone else. Don't even bother.**

In Irv Yalom's book, Love's Executioner,[27] the author, a distinguished Stanford psychiatrist and talented writer, relates a case study which highlights why therapy is not possible with someone who is in love. In so doing, he also shows that because the NEA affects rational judgment and attachments, anyone in this state is unreachable and simply not amenable to influence. No-one will give up a NEA willingly.

Commitment means having to tolerate frustration. Commitment means closing your mind to any exits. Egomaniacs don't make commitment because they cannot - will not - accept restraints. They do not want to be confined. It's all too easy to seek exits when the relationship is in turmoil. A motel room, a friend's house, your mother's, a friend's arms, the divorce court all might seem appealing when you are not getting what you want out of your partner. Although these sanctuaries *sometimes* have value as temporary solutions especially to avoid violence (see the chapter on Fighting Fair), they are also dangerous anti-commitment magnets that seduce you away from your promises to your partner. Would commitment be stronger if there were fewer exits? Suppose there was no divorce court? Or there were no convenient places of refuge? Would people try harder to maintain and repair their marriages?

The Origins of Commitment

Commitment is the ability to make an agreement and stick to it. Like every other important feature of human nature, this ability is learned in childhood. It is learned in two ways. First, it is learned by the treatment children themselves receive from their parents and caretakers in their early years. It is also learned by observing how the significant adults in their life act towards each other.

Parents and caretakers often don't mean what they say. In an effort to appease, reward or punish a child they will make statements that they do not back up with action. This is easily done. When a five-year-old is acting out of control and not responding to reasonable requests to calm down it is easy to say things like, "If you carry on like that you will not get any Christmas presents," (or dinner, or a birthday

---

[27] Irv Yalom, Love's Executioner, Harper, New York, 1989.

party or etc.,). Sometimes the child will respond to these threats. Often they won't because they don't fully understand what you are threatening or they don't believe you. And they won't believe you if they call your bluff and you fail to live up to your threat. No matter how much back-peddling you do (e.g. "after further consideration you will get Christmas presents because you have been good by (fill in the blank).."), the fact is that you took a position and then did not follow through on it. When I point out this fundamental dynamic of parenting, some parents take it to mean that they now have to impose their Draconian threats. That's not the answer at all. The answer is not to make outrageous threats to begin with, but stick to promising consequences that can be delivered.

Not all unfulfilled parental promises are threats. Sometimes events happen which make it impossible to follow through on a promise you fully intended to keep. You might have planned a family vacation, for example, and had to cancel it due to circumstances beyond your control. In this situation, explain to the child why this happened and arrange compensatory activity (e.g. another vacation at a different time) to uphold your promise. It is important for children to learn that events happen to pre-empt the best of plans.

If children observe their parents treating each other with respect, keeping promises and commitments, they, too, will develop this behavior. Not only do children observe their parents violating promises, sometimes they are put in the middle of the breach of loyalty. I have seen several cases where adolescents, sometimes even younger children, have had knowledge of one parent's extra marital affair and have been recruited to keep it a secret. It is hard to imagine a more divisive and destructive parental tactic. It is easy to see why such a behavior will create confusion, mistrust, suspicion and anger in a child.

Parents also teach commitment by ensuring that their children stick to the promises that they make. Children often say things to their friends, siblings and other children that they do not really mean or intend to follow through on. It is important for parents to ensure that this does not become a habit and that a child, if making a promise, keeps it.

Parental and family behavior are not the only important determinants of the ability to commit. There are also strong cultural messages about the nature of commitment and promise keeping. It is not uncommon, for example to hear about highly paid sports stars who wants to renegotiate a contract because another player has been able to strike a better deal. Commitment breaking and promise defaults have become epidemic in our society.

Consider the meteoric rise in the number of bankruptcies. In some cases, this is due to unfortunate and unforeseen circumstances that render a person helplessly incapable of meeting their financial obligations. In many other cases, however, this is a blatant and premeditated attempt to run up charges without having any inclination, let alone means, to repay these debts. This type of financial promise-breaking seems endemic in our society.

Commitment and childhood
How were you treated as a child?

Did parents/caretakers stick to their word?
Did parents/caretakers ensure you stuck to your promises?
Did parents/ caretakers make threats that they never carried out?
Did you know you could call parents/caretaker's bluff?

Difficulty Making Commitment

For some people, the difficulty in making a commitment is a reflection of a general indecision. These are people who cannot make a commitment to anything and they flit through life jumping indecisively from one activity to another, from one relationship to another. This inability to settle on a school, a career or a partner, can be a result of many factors like low self-esteem, depression, or immaturity.

There are also people who, while generally not indecisive, cannot make a commitment to an intimate relationship. Some people are afraid to commit because they realize that such a commitment involves the very steps described in this book, and they are not ready to meet those demands. The perceived loss of independence, power and control is sometimes magnified to such a degree that it becomes daunting. In a 1994 paper,[28] Curtis and Susman showed that fears about loss of identity, control and money as well as fears of adult responsibility are factors associated with fears about marriage. How satisfactorily these concessions can be negotiated and overcome will depend on each unique partnership.

Often, however, the difficulty committing comes from the fear of vulnerability. Commitment involves emotional exposure and the possibility of rejection and even abandonment. For those who are insecure about their own worth and lovability, such vulnerability can be too daunting to embrace. Others have attachment difficulties (described in more detail in Step 7) which make it difficult for them to really connect to another person. Most of the time, however, difficulty committing is a result of low self-esteem.

It is a truism that you have to love yourself to be able to love another.[29] If you do not love and value yourself you will view anyone expressing love to you as themselves flawed, having poor judgment and problematic. Alternatively, you will choose partners who reinforce your negative view of yourself and show it with abusive behavior. In time, many people will learn to abandon abusive partners but the insecurity and low self-esteem remain, trapping their owners in commitment limbo.

None of us receive the unconditional love for which we crave (except in the Novel Erotic Attachment, as described earlier). As a result, we are often afraid to extend ourselves in love. Making a commitment is making oneself vulnerable and there can be no cast-iron guarantees that such vulnerability won't be betrayed.

---

[28] Factors related to fear of marriage. Psychological Reports, 1994 Jun;74(3 Pt 1):859-863
[29] Loving yourself involves many of the *10 Steps* described in this book. Commitment to yourself, acceptance of strengths and weaknesses, trust in yourself and your intuition, nurturing, understanding, forgiveness (especially important in self-love) are all important determinants of how you treat and see yourself.

Commitment and Resolution

Commitment is one of the key determinants of success in couples therapy. For example, a young couple came with problems that were presenting as sexual. She wanted sex more frequently and too often felt rebuffed by her partner. He claimed the she was too demanding. This issue was creating much anger and frustration. Despite these difficulties, this couple still retained an essential respect for each other, were both willing to accept some responsibility for the situation and agreed that the *relationship was going to continue no matter what*. They were both so totally committed to the relationship that it was inevitable that they would come to an amicable solution. By being clear in their commitment, they avoided threatening postures that are so destructive and were able to focus all of their energy on actively seeking a solution rather than simply protecting their egos.

In my counseling with couples, I try to get a commitment from each partner that, for the duration of therapy, neither one of them make threats about leaving the relationship, divorcing or separating. At times of tension these feelings are common, but their expression is detrimental to therapy and frequently sabotages it. I can find no data on this subject but my strong suspicion is that success of therapy and reconciliation is directly related to the lack of such threats.

In a society were divorce is not only easy but half-expected, commitment has become a brittle concept.

> **Commitment is like a limb of a tree: it thrives when it is sunny and warm but snaps and breaks in icy conditions.**

Focus On The Relationship

We all know people who seem to ooze commitment. They do everything with a single-minded focus and they do it 110%. There is no doubt about their level of involvement in the task. Others seem so laid back and lackadaisical that they give the impression that they don't really care whether they are involved in the particular activity. So here's a good question to ask yourself.

Am I participating in this relationship 110%?

This will no doubt be followed quickly by another question that will occur to you.

Is my partner involved in this relationship 110%?

110% Participation

Physically and emotionally available

Relationship has priority

Relationship is always in the front of your mind

The movie, 'The Karate Kid'[30] is about commitment. In the movie an old Japanese-American caretaker, Mr. Miyagi, teaches Daniel, a teenager, the art of karate. At the beginning of his training, Daniel is not too sure that he really wants to learn karate, or at least learn the way Mr. Miyagi wants to teach it. In one memorable scene, Mr. Miyagi says to Daniel..

"Walk on right side of road.. safe. Walk on left side of road.. safe. Walk in middle of road.. squished like grape."

Whether it is karate, sport, academics, relationships or anything else, if you walk in the middle of the road, sooner or later, you are going to get squished like grape.

Being half-hearted in a relationship creates all sorts of problems. First, lack of commitment is easily sensed by partners. This is going to make them mad. We want full participation and commitment and anything less is going to hook our insecurities about not measuring up. Making a partner mad and insecure is not a smart thing to do if you want to retain a good union. Lack of commitment is likely to engender not only feelings of anger, but withdrawal. A loss of intimacy, declining sexual relations, increased tension and hostility will eventually emerge where one partner is only partially committed.

---

[30] The Karate Kid, Columbia Pictures. Screenplay by Robert Mark Kamen.

In a paper that was commissioned by an educational foundation,[31] I researched the factors responsible for success. I found that the biggest key to success in any endeavor is perseverance. No matter how much talent or other advantages you have going, in the end success will be determined by your determination. I have met many successful entrepreneurs and people from all walks of life and they all said the same thing - success takes time. None of these successful people would have ever reached their goals if they had lost interest, or stopped believing in what they were doing. Relationships are no exception.

Commitment is easy when things are going great - who would not want to stick around a successful show. It is not so easy to make that commitment when the relationship is in trouble - but *that is just the time when commitment needs to be reinforced.* There may be no more powerful message to your partner than a reaffirmation of your commitment when things are not going well, as the following case history suggests.

John is a supervisor at a manufacturing plant. His wife of thirteen years, Bridget is an accomplished music teacher with distinctive features and flaming red hair. Bridget has suffered with depression at various times in her life. Four years ago, Bridget's depression re-emerged with a vengeance, for no apparent reason. It was into the blues from out of the blue, so to speak. She was this time diagnosed with a bipolar depression and prescribed powerful anti-depressive medication.

People with bipolar depression suffer from hopelessness, loss of energy and irritability. Bridget went through periods of being able to function fairly well and periods where her judgment and decision making were appalling. John had to clear up the fall-out from her inappropriate behavior. Intimacy evaporated. John was having to run the family, bail Bridget from out of her adventures and try to lead a normal life of his own.

---

[31] "Success", commissioned by the Hite Foundation in March 1990

After many months of this erratic and exhausting life, many partners could be forgiven for wanting to give up. During one session, Bridget herself volunteered, "I wouldn't blame you if you wanted a divorce. I would hate that but I would understand it."

John was clearly considering separation as one of his options when one night he had the following dream that he reported in detail at our next session.

"There was this fire in a building - it could have been our house - I am not sure. I managed to escape the flames and made it out into the front yard. I remember feeling very frightened and agitated. The firemen had just arrived when I remembered that I had some very important notes in the building that I had to retrieve. I knew I had to go back into the building. The fireman tried to restrain me. They were telling me I must not go but somehow I got passed them and reentered the flames. Things were crashing down about me everywhere but I felt a strange sense of calm - as if I knew I was meant to be there. At that moment I was not concerned about living or dying. Although there was choking black smoke everywhere I reached the notes. The next thing I remember was that the heat had dissipated and I could hear one of the fireman say that the flames were being brought under control."[32]

During the same session that John related this dream he announced that he had decided that separation was not a viable option for him. He told Bridget, in front of me, that he was staying with her no matter what.

The next few weeks and months continued to be difficult, although much of the tension had been reduced by John's decision. Eventually, Bridget's depression was brought under control and she and John were able to resurrect the relationship - even stronger than before.

---

[32] I let you interpret this one. But in case you missed it at least look at the connection between Bridget's "flaming red hair" and the fire, and her musical talent and her husband's search for notes.

No-one could have blamed John if he had decided that he had reached the limits of his capacities and decided to terminate the relationship. There are times when staying together seriously jeopardizes the well-being of one or more individuals. Under these conditions separation or divorce have to be seriously considered, preferably with prior work with a trained counselor. When to seek help and even terminate a relationship is discussed more fully in the chapter on Getting Help.

Commitment Enhancers
There are some actions that you can do to increase commitment. These actions range from simple, occasional behaviors to fundamental principles.

One of fundamental principles is to avoid unilateral action. Seeking mutual agreement and not acting until it has been achieved is a positive sign of commitment. This may slow down some decision-making but it is better to move forward together slowly, than move quickly apart. Unilateral decisions lead to trouble, especially if they are about important issues.

A husband gets the offer of a transfer to a better corporate job in another city. His wife however, is very settled where she is, with a good social circle, family and a lifestyle she likes. How do they go about resolving this problem?

Unilateral action by either of them is not the best solution. If the husband assumes that his wife will follow him without question or complaint she is for ever going to be resentful and probably will never settle in her new town. If the wife assumes that she is going to stay put, the husband will resent her obstruction to his career.

This problem is common and is not just about relocation. There are many ways of resolving this particular dispute. The best ways involve communication and addressing the deeper underlying issues; *power, control* and *hope*.

The problem with a one-sided dictate is that makes your partner feel unappreciated and powerless. There is much greater chance for an amicable solution by giving your partner some control and power over the decision. Those couples who resolve their dilemmas in this way have happier relationships.

In the relocation dilemma, there are many possible solutions. In some cases, the husband agrees to "go on ahead" for a period of a few months to ensure that he is settled before uprooting his family. In other cases, a spouse might agree to go, given assurances that she can have a generous travel allowance to maintain contacts in her current city. The couple might decide to reject the transfer and stay put. From the point of view of the relationship, *the decision itself does not matter, it is the way that it is derived that is important.*

Resisting the temptation to take one-sided action is not only important in a healthy relationship, but is also critical when things don't work out. One of the problems in a relationship break-up is that the anger polarizes the individuals and they stop acting with respect towards each other. More and more unilateral actions are taken, the parties become more polarized and the lawyers get rich.

The most amicable divorces and break-ups I have observed come when the parties manage to retain their respect for each other and do not take unilateral action. No significant action is taken without mutual agreement. This sometimes can make for a slower separation but it always makes for a less painful experience and one which allows the parties to retain a cordial relationship.

Commitment Exercises

A marriage is a contract. Most people don't think of it in those terms because they are never asked to sign a legal document that accurately summarizes their marital duties and obligations, which are generally discussed in the most abstract terms.

- Putting a commitment in writing and signing it, then having it duly notarized makes the commitment tangible and thus seem more real.[33]

---

[33] Consult a lawyer if you are unsure of the implications of your action. Seeking legal advice before signing anything is a good general rule.

- Draw up a document which summarizes your commitment to each other. Itemize the actions to which you are committing. You might even agree to waive some of the grounds for divorce. For example, in Louisiana, it is possible to sign a four year agreement in which both parties renounce their ability to divorce during the period of the contract except on the grounds of physical abuse.

- If the above is too drastic for you, just writing down a list of responsibilities is a useful activity. At the very least, renew your marriage vows.

Step Four

Trusting

Trust permeates a relationship. We make assumptions about our partner's actions, thoughts and feelings that affect every aspect of the relationship. We trust that our partners are telling us what we need to know and doing what they say they are doing. There are two sides to this particular coin - the ability to trust and the ability to be trustworthy.

Implicit trust assumptions in relationships

Partners have a right to expect the other to..

Speak the truth
Volunteer the truth
Be factually accurate about whereabouts, activities, money
Openly express feelings
Inform of important events that affect the relationship and each others' lives

---

Trust is based on your life experience and the unique experience within the relationship. Lack of trust is corrosive. It eats away at the very fabric of a relationship and leads to disillusion and dissolution. Once trust has been broken, it is very difficult, often impossible, to regain it. Even a gullible person will wise up eventually to an untrustworthy partner. It might take them some time - but they will eventually.

Never violate trust

Trust, Reliability and Predictability

We don't like to be shocked or surprised - except under certain controlled settings, like the amusement park or the movies. Otherwise, uncertainty is unsettling and anxiety-provoking. That does not mean that life has to be boring and humdrum. In small superficial ways, variety is indeed the spice of life. On the big things, however, - like loyalty, integrity, fairness, honesty - we do much better when we know where we stand. Being deceived by someone whom we thought trustworthy threatens our whole view of our world, including ourselves. This one factor alone causes justifiable anger and rage in those who have been deceived by a partner. If you have ever had this experience you will know how unnerving it is. Suddenly, you realize how much of life is based on unverified assumptions of predictability and reliability.

Untrustworthiness

Untrustworthiness comes in different shapes and sizes and for different reasons. It is not the case that just because someone is untrustworthy in one situation that they will be in all situations. Research and experience suggests that untrustworthiness is a personality trait for some, and a situation-specific behavior for others.

Untrustworthiness is manifested in three main ways.

1. Shame and embarrassment cause a person to be defensive and deceitful about their behavior. This leads to a trail of deceit to cover-up the original problem. Individuals with impulse control difficulties have this problem in a big way. Compulsive gambling, shopping, eating, drinking and drug abuse all create this pattern of deceit and untrustworthiness. The addict who gets caught in a growing web of deceit is no different than the non-addict in the same situation. Addiction has come to mean, in its broadest terms, this pattern of behavior and the term "addict" has become synonymous with someone who demonstrates these problems. Addiction, however, is a subset of human behavior, not the other way round. It is human nature to attempt to conceal shameful and embarrassing acts. An individual trying to conceal an act of infidelity, for example, will act the same way even though they are not addicted (unless they make infidelity a habit). Anyone who has ever lived with an addict will know how difficult it is to trust the addict's pledge that they will never indulge in alcohol, drugs or gambling again. One of the commonest difficulties in recovery is the restoration of trust.

2. In the above example, embarrassment, shame and guilt lead to deceitful and untrustworthy behavior, typically as a result of

impulse control problems. At least these people experience shame, guilt and embarrassment. There are another group who do not experience such emotions and their untrustworthiness stems from their inability or reluctance to empathize with anyone, not even their partners. People who have such psychopathic personalities withhold information and are selective with the truth. They will say and do anything to get their way. They are completely unreliable and dangerous - often physically as well as emotionally. Narcissists exhibit this behavior. Their own self-aggrandizement is so consuming that they will exploit anything and anyone to fan, what under all their bluster, is a very fragile ego. Unfortunately we live in such a society that accepts a means-justifies-the-ends philosophy so we should not be surprised that this type of behavior flourishes.

3. The third group who are prone to violating trust are those people-pleasers who cannot tolerate conflict or confrontation. Their inability to face the sometimes difficult consequences of addressing reality results in deceit and eventual untrustworthiness. They tell their partners what they think their partners want to hear. They will stretch the truth to cover their oversized desire to avoid conflict.

If you have a relationship with a personality-disordered individual who is incapable of empathy and trust you have major problems and not much of a relationship. If you have a relationship with an addictive personality not only do they need to abandon their addiction but they also need to deal with their embarrassment, shame and guilt. If you have a relationship with a people-pleaser, lucky you. Well, not really. Ultimately their inability to be honest will outweigh any benefits you get from their insatiable desire to please.

Trust and Honesty
Being honest is not just about not telling a lie. Honesty is about maintaining the spirit and integrity of your relationship. For example, a man once confided in my that he had an affair. I asked him whether his wife knew. He claimed she did not and became upset when I called him dishonest. "I never lied to her," he objected, "she never asked me if I was having one." Obviously, dishonesty is about violating the tacit agreements in your relationship, whether you speak about them openly or not.

The problem with dishonesty is that once you have lost trust it takes a lot of time and bridge-building to restore it. Even then, you cannot eradicate experience. Once you have implanted the feeling of doubt and suspicion in your partner's mind you will never get it out. They might learn to deal with it and minimize it but the experience will be encoded forever in their nervous system.

Trust and Fidelity

Although trust impinges on every aspect of the relationship, fidelity is typically the subject of most concern. Sex not only is your most intimate act, it is also a symbol of your special union. In an era of AIDS and other sexually transmitted diseases, medical considerations have also become very important. Infidelity typically leads to massive, often lethal, relationship problems. In one study the disclosure of infidelity led to divorce in 34% of the cases and a worse relationship in 44% of cases. In 14% of the cases, the incident was the catalyst for work that ultimately improved the relationship.[34]

Extramarital sex is more than just a little rash

It is part of human nature that men and women are attracted to each other. In the earlier chapters I emphasized the powerful genetic force that attracts men and women and this does not simply disappear once you are in a committed relationship. Even when married it is inevitable that you will find other people attractive and you might even be irresistibly drawn to them. The main purpose of this book is to show that such feelings are not love. Just because you feel such emotions, however, does not mean that you have to act out on them. There is nothing wrong with finding another person attractive and even experiencing strong attraction. What matters is how you are able to manage those feelings.

Your partner will take his or her lead on how much trust they have from you. If you do not trust yourself to effectively manage

---

[34] Charny IW, Parnass S., The impact of extramarital relationships on the continuation of marriages, in Sex & Marital Therapy, 1995;21(2):100-115.

intimate advances from others, doubt will be created in your partner's mind. Handling intimate interest and sexual advances is a challenge that many feel is beyond their impulse control skills. As a result they take steps to avoid such a situation by minimizing social contact, keeping their distance in interpersonal relationships outside of marriage, or doing things that they believe make them unattractive (e.g. gaining weight).

Restoring Trust

Although trust is very difficult to restore, human beings are remarkably sensitive to the present. They have to be to survive. Even if you have a relationship with a forty-year history of honesty and complete trust and this is violated, enough doubt and suspicion, not to mention anger, have been introduced to virtually eradicate all of that good past history. On the flip side, it does mean, however, that it is possible to restore trust. In order to regain trust a partner has to…

- Stop the untrustworthy behavior

- Be open and honest about any offending behavior

- Understand that forgiveness and the restoration of trust will take time

- Apologize

- Empathize with the partner's hurt

- Make amends

How much do you trust your partner to act appropriately in the following areas? (Mark anywhere on the dotted line)

Sex
No trust at all |..| Complete trust

Money
No trust at all |..| Complete trust

Family
No trust at all |..| Complete trust

Friends
No trust at all |..| Complete trust

You(Respectfully handle your feelings, thoughts etc.)
No trust at all |..| Complete trust

How much do you trust yourself to act appropriately in the following areas? (Mark anywhere on the dotted line)

Sex
No trust at all |..| Complete trust

Money
No trust at all |..| Complete trust

Family
No trust at all |..| Complete trust

Friends
No trust at all |..| Complete trust

You(Respectfully handle your feelings, thoughts etc.)
No trust at all |..| Complete trust

The Origins of Trust

The ability to trust, like all important behaviors, is based on experience, especially childhood experience. Trustworthy, consistent parents instill a sense of trust. By acting reliably and predictably they reassure children that key figures say what they mean and mean what they say. Children in such families learn that their parents can be relied upon to keep them safe. Overprotective parents often don't instill trust. There is a danger that by protecting a child too much, such parents don't teach the appropriate boundaries of trust. A child of such parents might not learn that some people can be trusted while others cannot. He or she may learn to be too trusting, thus risking naïveté and gullibility.

Unreliable parents raise untrusting children. Excessive teasing and games that some parents misperceive as harmless can destroy trust. I have seen children whose parents were always playing tricks on them, develop into paranoid individuals who find it difficult to trust. Anyone raised in an unsafe environment where they might be betrayed at any moment is obviously going to have difficulty trusting.

Trusting Intuition

One other way that trust impinges on your relationship is the trust you have in yourself, specifically your judgment and intuition. Many have not learned to trust their intuition. It is not that your intuition is always right. Thoughts and feelings should rarely be accepted without verification and analysis. Thoughts, however, should always be listened to and explored. They may not be accurate. They may, for example, simply be echoes of neuroticism or sensitivity that are difficult to completely discard. So always listen to your intuition but *accept* it only after you have considered it carefully.

Fall-Out From Mistrust

The fall-out from broken trust is withdrawal, alienation, anger and almost inevitably a loss of intimacy. It leads to control, dependency and rage.

Jealousy can literally kill a relationship. Morbid jealousy, especially in combination with alcohol or drug use, is responsible for many homicides and suicides. Jealousy is more dangerous when it is part of the individual's personality rather than a response to a mate's unfaithful and untrustworthy behavior. Nonetheless, all jealousy undermines a partnership. The jealous person often will go to extreme lengths to prove their suspicions and prevent what they consider to be untrustworthy and unfaithful behavior.

If your partner has a jealous and possessive personality it is going to be difficult if not impossible to change them. Such people will try to control and hang on to you as if their life depended on it - which in a way it does.

I have a distant female relative who is extraordinarily talented and attractive. As a junior in high school she was picked up by a man several years her senior and they began a relationship, much to the chagrin of her family. The man kept tight control on the girl. After a couple of years, the girl admitted that she wanted to break the relationship but was too scared to do so. The family helped her and one of her brothers gave her a safe haven in his home. The boyfriend tracked her down and asked only that he could talk to her. On being allowed into the house, he cut the telephone line and started chasing people around with a large knife. The police were called and he escaped. He returned an hour later and only by pure luck was he spotted entering the house. It took eight policemen to hold him down. A restraining order was issued that he largely ignored. He made threats against the family. The girl ran away to Europe - the man tracked her down. The girl ran away to Australia - the man tracked her down. This happened seventeen years ago. Last time I heard, they were still together.

Trust Exercises
The restoration of trust is possible but it takes time and involves forgiveness (see Step 9). Even in circumstances where mistrust has not occurred there are behaviors that can maintain and develop a trusting relationship.

- Communication builds trust. Establishing the habit of sharing thoughts and feelings and having them accepted is essential. A lot of mistrust is a result of poor communication. Communicating and agreeing about shared expectations, roles and goals minimizes potential confusion and feelings of betrayal.

- Create an environment where trust is possible and honesty is rewarded. Mistrustful people think they are going to be tricked. You always have to be perfectly plain and clear in your communication to such a person to minimize hooking their paranoia. You won't be able to eradicate all suspicion, but you can certainly reduce it.

- Learn how to deal with anger. If you can manage anger and resolve disputes you are less likely to resort to lies and deceit to avoid it. Techniques for dealing with anger are discussed on page 162.

Step Five

Sharing

Sharing is an essential part of any healthy relationship. If you cannot share, you cannot give. If you cannot give, you cannot love.

Sharing involves stepping outside the boundaries of possessiveness. I was once in a restaurant with a group of friends, one of whom was a young woman I did not know very well. The server was being typically sociable and was particularly enamored of the pendant that the young woman was wearing. It was clear that the waitress was not just making small talk - she really did like the piece of jewelry. The meal passed uneventfully, with the waitress providing good, if unspectacular, service. At the end of the meal, the young woman removed her pendant, scribbled a short note and left the piece of jewelry for the waitress on the table.

When the group found out what had happened we were aghast. This was not the most expensive piece of jewelry but it did not come from the dollar store either. The event was the talking point of the evening. Why had she done it? Being the supposed expert in human behavior, I was asked all sorts of questions. What was the psychological explanation for this behavior? Was she suffering from some type of psychological disorder, and if so, what?

For a while I contemplated these questions as eagerly as they were asked. This young woman had given a piece of jewelry, that she liked enough to wear, to a complete stranger that she probably would never see again. The young woman was not especially wealthy. What was remarkable was that the donor did not seem to want anything in return - not even the satisfaction of seeing the waitress find her unexpected gift. She had no special affinity to the server and was not trying to impress the group. In fact, she was somewhat embarrassed by the stir her action had caused. She did not see anything out of the ordinary with her action.

There *was* something extraordinary about her behavior - most people don't give perfectly good possessions to which they have some attachment to complete strangers, especially when they act as if they want nothing in return.

I thought about what had happened for a long time. I came to the conclusion that this was just one enormous act of generosity and I felt some guilt and embarrassment that I had even briefly considered the action a psychiatric symptom. This young woman, had simply indulged in the supremely satisfying act of sharing. I have to admit to feeling a little sad that such behavior was so unusual that a group of intelligent people questioned its sanity.

In contemporary society we are not very good at sharing. We are a consumer society that values possessions and possessing. We fight hard for ownership and can't let go. We are so consumed with acquisition that the reverse is too jarring to contemplate. You only need to look in the typical attic to see how difficult it is for people to let go. Most of us carry around the flotsam of our lives forever. Admittedly some of this flotsam has emotional value but as lot of it is just junk. We just can't let it go.

On those occasions where we give something up, we want - demand - something in return. Even charitable giving has to be encouraged by providing a tax break to the donor. Unconditional giving is alien. In a commerce oriented, consumer society such an ethos is understandable. It just does not lend itself very well to the development of sharing.

We all want unconditional love but find it very difficult to give unconditionally. Sharing is unconditional giving. If you are going to share but expect something in return you are not really sharing, you are trading.

When was the last time you did something for your partner unconditionally?

Some of the things that are shared in a healthy relationship:

Time

Money

Possessions

Family

Friends

Power

Secrets

Experiences

Dreams

What other things do you share?

If a person cannot share then it is not possible for them to really love. Sharing requires respect and teamwork. Every couple needs some shared activities otherwise intimacy is not possible. Often, when a couple are struggling to regain intimacy, I will encourage them to simply spend a few minutes together in a joint activity. As outlined in the chapter on romancing, doing anything together is an act of intimacy.

Fred and Nancy are a professional couple who have steadily drifted apart. They live their lives in a quiet, mutual but distant respect. They organize their lives independently and divide household chores and tasks evenly. Intimacy has evaporated with time. As I explore their world, I discover that there is not one thing that do together. They organize their time so that each partner can follow their own independent paths without disrupting their family too much. They are so addicted to independence that they suggest that I see them each in individual therapy. I refuse to do this, offering only to see them as a couple and thus ensuring that at least for an hour a week they are participating in a joint activity.

I organize their appointments in the evening so they have to get a baby-sitter. With this arrangement in place, I suggest that they might like to follow the pattern of many of my clients and take the time after the session to have a quiet dinner together. During our sessions I encourage discussion about each of their own dreams and hopes, pointing out the numerous similarities in their aspirations. I take every opportunity to encourage them subtly to do joint activities. If they are planning to come to the session in two separate cars, I encourage them to travel together in one car. Gradually, as they learn to share their time with each other, communication improves, friendship grows and their intimacy returns.

Reluctant Receivers

Sharing is about receiving as well as giving. Some people find it difficult to receive because they have such low self-esteem that they don't believe they are worthy of the gift. Receiving something unconditionally challenges their predominant sense of worthlessness and elicits tremendous discomfort. It is far easier for them to reject the giving than change their self-concept.

Other people are reluctant receivers because they are very suspicious of unconditional gifts. They have a history of never having received anything unconditionally or, more likely, previous resources given unconditionally turned out not to be unconditional at all. They may have, for example, been raised in homes where parents offered love or money on unconditional grounds, only to have the gift held over them, like the sword of Damocles, at a later date.

In a relationship the ability to receive is as important as the ability to give. If you cannot receive, your partner cannot give. Not only are you depriving your partner of an important source of pleasure, you are damaging the relationship.

The Origins Of Sharing

Like every other trait that is essential for a good intimate relationship, sharing is learned in childhood. Some children are encouraged to share, others are not. I know families where a competitive, uncompromising no sharing attitude is encouraged by parents in the mistaken belief that this will better prepare their child for the harsh realities of the real world. All it does is ensure that the child develops into a lonely adult who never understands or knows the joy of giving.

It is often assumed that the only child will not learn to share because they do not have to. Many only children are very capable and happy to share because they have been taught to do so, they have seen it in their parents and are secure enough to give up part of what they have. More typically, children in large families have difficult sharing because there is such a premium on their resources that they are unprepared to give them up when they do get them.

I have a vivid recollection of an early personal encounter with sharing. I must have been about two and a half. We were living in London, and my mother and sister and I were walking home from a shopping expedition. About half-a mile from our home, a huge thunderstorm broke. Massive hailstones started to rain down, the wind picked up and the thunder started to crack over head. As this weather event was developing, my mother grabbed me by the hand, knocking to the ground a packet of my favorite sugar coated snacks that I was lovingly holding. I looked back and saw the beloved packet of snacks carried on a torrent of water, inexorably and inconsolably sailing towards the storm drain. My mother grabbed me once more and before long we arrived home just in time to sense a blinding flash and a thunderous crack that split a tree in our backyard in two. Something big was happening.

We were relieved to make it inside. My mother got some towels and as we were drying off my sister (nearly four years my senior) opened her hand to reveal her packet of snacks, exactly the same kind that I had lost. She had been able to hang on to hers. She opened the bag and proceeded to lay out everyone of the snacks. After counting them, she divided them equally and gave me half.

Whether it was the excitement of our brush with the elements or the fact that the storm was raging outside or something else, I was very moved by my sister's gesture. She did not do it grudgingly, she did not ask for anything in return, she did not have to be prompted. She just shared.

The Value of Sharing

Human beings are social animals. In our society which focuses on individual talents and achievements and is based on the concept of individual freedom, it is easy to underestimate the fact that we live in a social world. Other people are essential to our survival. Other people give our life meaning.

Some years ago I was counseling a depressed, lonely woman. She seemed to be immovably stuck. I was wondering what on earth could be done to shake her depression. One day she arrived at my office looking completely different. There was a spring in her step. She wore colorful clothes rather than her usual drab outfits, she wore a smile rather than her usual drab expression. I could not imagine what could have happened to transform lethargy and hurt into vitality.

What happened is that she had an opportunity to share. A long lost relative had called and was in need of companionship during a convalescence. Now, at last, my client had found meaning and purpose. Sharing herself gave her life.

Sharing, Social Interaction and Health

Biological evidence confirms the critical role of relationships for health and functioning. There is much research evidence showing that isolated people are less healthy, both physically and mentally. There are gender differences in these findings. Generally, women have and require more social ties than men. But both genders are adversely influenced by social isolation. There are also a number of studies that show isolation lowers the body's immune system.

Robert Sapolsky, a leading researcher from Stanford,[35] has extensively studied primates, social animals like humans. His research

---

[35] For those interested in a very readable and informative book on stress and how it effects the immune system, check out Saplosky's "Why Zebras Don't Get Ulcers," Freeman, New York, 1994

has shown that when primates are in social and physical contact, their heart rate goes down - in other words, they become more relaxed. Moreover, when the primates are in social interaction, their immune system becomes stronger. At least for these social animals, then, social interaction is associated with optimum health.

Studies with humans show similar results. In a 1997 study, Dr Sheldon Cohen and his colleagues[36] showed that resistance to cold viruses was significantly enhanced by the number of social ties. People with more types of social connection were less likely to develop cold symptoms when injected with rhinoviruses. This suggests that, to a point, the more social contacts a person has, the more resistant to disease they are.

Research also shows what most of know from experience and intuitively expect; that people who become isolated, (for example by the death of a spouse) have an increased risk of disease and death. The relationship between stress and disease is complex. While it is known that stress can result in the suppression of the immune system, we do not know for sure how much of an effect this really is. For example, although the disease and death rate does increase following loss of a spouse, there may be contributing factors other than stress. We know that medical care and support, things like taking medications and getting to the doctor, also reduce after spousal loss and this may be as big a factor in increased disease risk as the biological effects of loss on the immune system.

Sharing Exercises

Here are some things that you can do to sharpen your ability to share.
- **Unconditionally give your time**. Each partner agree to give a couple of hours over to do something your partner elects to do - even if it is not something you particularly want to do. Once in a while both (or the whole family) of you spend some time donating your time to a charitable cause. When you are doing these activities, give your time

---

[36] Journal of the American Medical Association, 1997, 277, 1940 - 1944

willingly and be open-minded. Approach the time spent as an opportunity for a new experience and look for the positive aspects and the meaning that can be derived from participating.

- **Unconditionally give money.** Donate an affordable amount of money to a charity that you have never given to before.

- **Unconditionally give possessions.** Find a possession that you can bear to part with and donate it to somebody or some organization.

Step Six

Fighting Fair

Conflicts and disagreements are inevitable in a long term relationship so how these are handled are critical. If you can't handle the conflicts, your relationship won't survive.

What Couples Argue About

On the surface it would appear that couples argue most about money and sex. But are these disputes really about sex and money or are they about something else? Emotional discussions, by their very nature, are about more important underlying issues, like trust, control, jealousy etc. A dispute about where to go on vacation, how much to spend for Christmas or where the kids should go to school will not escalate into an argument unless it reflects a more fundamental issue. Arguments about money and sex are mostly about control. Money and sex are the currency of control in many relationships. Withholding sex is a classic way partners, both male and female, use to assert control.

The issue at the heart of most conflict, therefore is control. How you handle these conflicts will determine whether the underlying problem is exacerbated or resolved.

A couple who had been married for four years sought help from me. The wife was the prime mover in seeking treatment. Her complaint was about her husband's financial irresponsibility. She worked in a manufacturing plant and he was self-employed. Her income was stable and predictable, his was more variable. Although he contributed to the household expenses, the responsibility of financial management fell to her. The first session or two was taken up with her complaint about his lack of a *predictable* contribution. So we painstakingly drew up a budget, divided it into half and secured the man's agreement to met these obligations each week.

The experienced observer of human nature will recognize, however, that this was not the end of the problem. Despite the fact that her husband broadly stuck to the agreement (the timing of his paychecks made this difficult in practice, but he observed the spirit of the agreement), she was still not satisfied. Now she was unhappy with the way he divided his time and before long it was obvious that the initial dispute had not really been about money at all. It was about her insecurity bred by her husband's apparent lack of commitment. In her view, he was not pulling his weight, either in financial or time commitment. The more she pressed him on this the more he saw her as attempting to control him, the more reluctant he became to commit his resources the way she wanted. And so the dance went on.

There are ways to argue constructively and fight fairly regardless of the latent or manifest content of your discussion. Having observed my fair share of marital arguments, I can tell you that there are specific tactics that escalate the fight and specific tactics that can resolve a fight.

Studies show that significant emotional arousal leads to physical changes during a fight even in long-term relationships. In one study[37], endocrine changes were measured during different, mainly negative, interactions in couples who had been together for an average of forty-two years. Interestingly these endocrine changes were related to the negativity of the argument in women but not in men. The researchers report that, "Both men and women who showed relatively poorer immunological responses displayed more negative behavior during conflict; they also characterized their usual marital disagreements as more negative than individuals who showed better immune responses across assays." The authors conclude that, "Abrasive marital interactions may have physiological consequences even among older adults in long-term marriages."

Managing the increases in stress and minimizing such physiological changes should be a goal when fighting. Once the situation has generated such a high level of tension that endocrine function is changing, it's time to cool down. The problem is really one

---

[37] Kiecolt-Glaser JK, Glaser R, Cacioppo JT, MacCallum RC, Snydersmith M, Kim C, Malarkey WB., Marital conflict in older adults: endocrinological and immunological correlates, in Psychosomatic Medicine, 1997 Jul;59(4):339-349

of escalation. Where at all possible, prevent the fight from spiraling out of control.

Knowledge makes your partner a formidable opponent. Partners know hot buttons and sensitivities and will be tempted to use them in a fight. A fight can also be the focus of all the other frustrations you have with your partner. All of your resentment for the things that you have accepted or sacrificed can find expression in an argument. It can also be the focus for your frustration and anger with the rest of the world.

I understand that fights are inevitable and that you are not always going to be able to exercise great self-control but if you can adopt some of the strategies identified below, you can keep arguing to a minimum and more importantly, argue more constructively. With that in mind, here are my tips for fighting fairly and more constructively.

The Not So Dirty Dozen: Twelve Rules For Fighting Fair
1. **Never resort to physical violence**. Physical violence is used by both men and women. Remember, how you express yourself is more important than what you say. If your express yourself violently or crudely any rational value your argument may have will be diluted, if not lost altogether. Few people will take someone who is out of control seriously. The medium is the message.

2. **Learn to call time-out or walk away if it's getting too hot**. There's no point continuing a discussion that is going nowhere. Escalation is going to lead to more emotion and arousal and less constructive interaction. Recognize when you are going into this danger zone. Make an agreement that either party can call a time-out, and this will be respected by the other person. Part of the agreement, however, is that the other partner can call for a re-opening of the discussion within twenty-four hours. This provides a cooling-off period but does not allow one partner to avoid the argument altogether.

3. **Be careful what you say.** Words can rarely be retracted. (The jury can't disregard that last statement and it will never be struck from the record.) Remember, people are not logical, they are emotional beings. Even if they know your insult was said in anger it will still penetrate their unconscious, have an impact and may influence them for years.

4. **Don't dredge up ancient history.** Memory erodes over time. Everyone will put the spin on events that is most favorable to them. It is also possible to take anything out of context and make yourself sound good. The real reasons people dredge up ancient history are..

- They have never resolved the original problem

- It is a similar example of what's really currently bothering them

- They don't have very much current ammunition

- They know it annoys the heck out of their partner and frankly, irritating them is the number one goal.

Dredging up ancient history is likely to lead to escalation. Either your partner will come back with some ancient history of his or her own..

"Yeah, and what about the time you …."

Alternatively, the history lesson will incite a review of your inadequacies..

"Haven't you gotten over that, yet..! Can't you ever let go of anything?"

Either way, as far as an argument is concerned, history is bunk.

5. **Try to resolve it yourselves.** Don't resort to a third party unless it's a professional. Seeking professional help

however. As outlined in the chapter on Getting Help, there is an enormous value in being able to review disputes in front of a professional. A different environment and an independent professional force you to curb some of the excesses of your anger.

Don't involve anyone other than a professional. Family members and friends cannot be unbiased and will be around after the dispute. They might be changed by the argument and besides, they probably don't want to get involved anyway.

6. **Fight in private.** Do not fight in front of the kids or anyone else. Even if you are not intending to enlist others to resolve disputes, try to avoid fighting in public. It's embarrassing to everyone, will affect your relationship with them and shows you have no control. In the same vein, be very careful about complaining about your spouse to friends and relatives. They are not objective and neither are you. You will inevitably provide a one-sided account, *your* account. That puts your friend in the unenviable position of questioning what you are saying, disagreeing with you or going along with you on the basis of a one-sided presentation.

Be careful about whom you confide in. It's difficult to find one reliable, helpful confidante, which is why there are people like me in business.

7. **Always apologize if you have stepped across the line**. There is a difference between your point of view and how that point of view is expressed. If you overreact, the danger is that your reaction rather than your position becomes the focus. In that way, overreacting jeopardizes your position because it detracts from it. Recognize and admit if you have got out of control and stepped across the line. That does not mean that your position is wrong, or that you have changed it.

Apologizing is an essential part of respecting your partners rights and boundaries so..

Love is having to say you're sorry

8. Don't argue or get into sensitive discussions, late at night, or when you are tired or have no energy for other reasons, e.g. sickness. Ideally, the purpose of a discussion is to resolve problems. As you have seen, conflict resolution requires active listening, frustration tolerance, self-control, compromise and diplomacy. All of these are in short supply when you are fatigued. Contrary to the myth that a couple should not go to bed angry, I believe it's better to go to bed angry and sleep on it, than try to resolve it when you don't have the resources and end up making matters worse.

9. Know when your partner is ready for the fight to be over. In time, you will learn the signals your partner uses to indicate a willingness to end the dispute. Conflicts should not be allowed to fester for days.

When not in a dispute, talk about the signals you each use to communicate you want the fight to be over.

10. Negotiate an outcome where both parties can save face. In his classic book "How To Win Friends and Influence People," Dale Carnegie[38] said "You can't win an argument." It's true. You might get a temporary sense of triumph but there is always a price to pay. Unlike other disputes in your life, you cannot easily avoid your spouse - you have to live with each other. This forces you to resolve problems. Those couples who spend much of their time apart are probably at a disadvantage here. You have to survive as a functioning unit, a fact which serves as motivation to end the dispute.

I once heard a negotiation described as similar to erecting a theater set on a stage. Different pieces of the set are put up by mutual agreement with both parties leaving enough space so

---

[38] Dale Carnegie, How to Win Friends and Influence People, Pocket Books, New York

that they can gracefully exit on their side of the stage. A satisfactory resolution of an argument allows for such a graceful and respected exit. If you are so egomaniacal that you always have to be right, or have the last word, or humiliate your partner, your relationship isn't going to last anyway.

11. Avoid the Reflected Accusation. The reflected accusation works like this. You are accused of a particular atrocity and instead of responding to the charge, you immediately accuse your partner of the very same crime. For example..

Partner A: I think you are being unfair!
Partner B: Oh, as if you are not unfair! What about last night when you...

This might be a great deflection device but it is sure to escalate the argument. A useful tactic for a person in a weak position but not helpful if you want to resolve a problem or restore harmony.

12. Avoid Interpretation. If you are really interested in good communication and resolving problems, avoid the interpretation of your partner's behavior. As I noted in the chapter on communication, interpreting your partner's behavior is only going to incite them more. Another good tactic for the person with a weak position.

Post-Fight Compensatory Closeness

A fight can end in closeness. When two people fight, they psychologically move apart from each other, stretching themselves away from each other like an elastic band. When the fight is over they are drawn back to each other, often with the same force of a stretched elastic band being released. This post-fight compensatory closeness generates feelings of acceptance and openness, especially if this feeling is being reciprocated. I had a friend who used this tactic to get better than average service in a restaurant. He would fabricate an argument with the server on his arrival but when he relented at strategically the right moment he found that the server's compensatory response included giving great service. A word of caution, however.

He was a master manipulator and this was in a different time and place. If you were to try that today chances are that you would either be bounced out of the restaurant or served last week's leftovers.

Post fight compensatory closeness does bring couples together. The one danger with this is that these post-fight feelings represent the closest times you have together. If this is the only time you feel close - or this is the time you feel closest - you might consciously or unconsciously start a fight to generate warm feelings! That's exactly what happened with one young couple. The wife was a generous, loving person; her husband was a big bore. In the first session, he himself admitted that he could be "a pain in the neck." In the second session, I thought he was more a pain in the rear. By the third session, I concluded that he was a pain at both ends of his spinal column.[39]

The problem was that he was an insecure and abrasive man who craved affection but would not venture out of his protective shell and risk vulnerability to get it. Consequently, he was continually frustrated, as was his poor, long-suffering wife. Arguments would naturally erupt. The phase of post-fight compensatory closeness was the only time he could feel safe enough to extend himself to get the love and attention he wanted. Her post-fight compensatory feelings of affection were actually reinforcing the arguments. He had developed a pattern where he would initiate a fight simply to get the affection at the end of it. This is obviously an unhealthy pattern and we worked long and hard on trying to get affection expressed at times other than at the end of a fight.

Learn from your fights. Learn what works, what is least destructive and restores order quickly. Learn know when to stop, when to call time-out, when to apologize and when simply to agree to differ.

---

[39] Therapists don't have to like their clients to be good counselors. A good therapist will be able to identify the patient characteristics that are turning them off, and once they have filtered out their own biases will use these patient characteristics as part of the therapeutic process. That is why a good professional counselor will have identified their own sensitivities and learned to manage them. Besides, a therapist's job is not to make friends with their clients, merely to help them. Ideally, a therapist should have no relationship with their clients other than a professional one.

Step Seven

Nurturing

Nurturing means accepting your partner's independence and doing whatever you can to encourage it. This requires you to feel comfortable in your own independence. If you are dependent you will be severely threatened by your partner's independence and do anything to prevent it. For this reason, dependent people have limited capacity to nurture.

Attachment

In recent years there has been increasing interest in the study of attachment. Attachment is the ability to form appropriate emotional and social bonds with other people, especially significant others. Much of the research has focused on children who seem to have this basic ability impaired. Sometimes this impairment is due to neglect and abandonment at an early age. Children who have spent time institutionalized from an early age, especially in developing countries or in countries at war, often have a profound disturbance of this essential human characteristic. Children who have biological developmental disorders like autism also have attachment problems.

The underlying characteristic of children with attachment difficulties is the absence of basic trust. This lack of trust creates feelings of isolation and "alone-ness". Such children feel as if they are different and have difficulty seeing themselves, and thus being, part of a social group. Such children also exhibit constant anger and have a tremendous need to be in total control. Many of these feelings are manifested in behavior directed specifically at the child's mother. Lack of eye contact and the inability to give and receive affection are other symptoms which can range from mild to severe. Attention Deficit Disorder is sometimes associated with this problem. No amount of love and affection can apparently satisfy children with attachment difficulties.

One severely attachment disordered child was described by her mother as "cruel to animals, defiant, hyperactive, senselessly destructive, forgetful, and a thief. People who don't know him well are instantly deceived. They see a handsome, charming, well-mannered, innocent, blue-eyed boy. This `innocent' intruder is sneaky, manipulative, superficial and always blames someone or something else for his problems. He rejects my efforts to care for him and has the uncanny knack for determining how to irritate me the most. There is no remorse when he does wrong."[40]

Conventional psychotherapy is not indicated for children with attachment disorders. Treatment for infants includes physical therapies that emphasize touch. Adolescents sometimes require residential treatment and/ or activity oriented adventure programs such as Outward Bound. It goes without saying that parenting such a child can be an immensely frustrating and difficult experience.

If the unattached child grows into an unattached adult, he or she will have serious interpersonal problems. Communicating, sharing, committing, forgiving - in fact all of the *10 Steps* - will be difficult for the person who has these problems, even to a moderate degree.

The child who has a healthy positive attachment to its parents, is able to eventually separate and develop as an individual Healthy children grow up and leave home eventually attaching to a partner and developing appropriate bonds to their own children.

What Is Healthy Attachment?

Attachment is a complex process by which parents and child develop a positive emotional connection. Attachment develops in three phases. In the first phase, the child develops trust in his or her parent. In the second phase bonds are formed through positive interaction between parent and child. The third phase involves the development of a sense of belonging.

We are first and foremost physical beings and our physical needs are paramount, especially in the first few months of life. Trust

---

[40] Huyser, N. Upside down and inside out. Family Bond-AID, (1996, March). pp. 1-2.

and bonding come directly from the experience of having our physical needs met. If we know that we will be fed when hungry, allowed to sleep when tired and changed when dirty we can develop a sense of control and trust.

Parents show their interest in the special nature of their child in their interactions. Whether that is playing, teaching or caring for physical needs these interactions communicate that we care and are the foundation of a special bond. In all of these activities, the parent makes themselves *emotionally available* to the child.

Once the child and parents mutually recognize that they have a special relationship, claiming and belonging occur. This is the core feeling of family and is based on this special feeling of togetherness.

Attachment and Adults
What can we learn about attachment in adult relationships from this work on attachment in children? I believe that we can see that the same three factors that develop attachment in children develop attachment in adults.

1. **A bond is formed by meeting needs**. In the infant, these needs are primarily physical. In the adult, these needs are both physical and psychological.

Although most adults are not dependent on others for food, warmth and shelter they are dependent on others for the gratification of physical needs. There is evidence that although they may not be as dependent as the infant for the basics of life, *quality* of lifestyle is a factor in attraction and mate selection. Research shows that the man's ability to provide for her and her children is a factor in women's mate selection. No doubt this is a throwback to a primitive age where the guy with the driest hut, or the warmest cave, or the most food was rated high on the eligibility list by the females in his tribe.

Men also select according to primitive needs. For the man, childbearing potential is a factor in attraction and mate selection. Given that males can procreate to a much later age in women, this phenomena goes some way to explaining why older men often select younger women. It may not be completely due to a mid-life crisis. Part of the male sex drive is mediated by a physiological drive, if not a conscious one, to procreate and thus will influence mate selection.

Which brings us back to sex and adult physical needs. Physical comfort, touching, caressing and sex are natural, important and primitive needs that are strong in most adults unless traumatic experience or disease has intervened to disrupt them. *Good sexual relations are important because in meeting each others physical needs, attachment is strengthened.* Attachment erodes in relationships were sex is infrequent or inadequate.

2. **The bond is strengthened through positive interchanges and emotional availability**. The first stage in the development of the child's bond is that physical needs are met reliably and predictably. The section on trust discussed the importance of these issues. Having needs satisfied is the first step, having appropriate positive emotional interchange is the second.

A robot could be trained to meet all the needs of a child - reliably and predictably. It just would not be much fun for the child. In fact, the child would have a pretty impoverished existence. One only needs to observe what happens to children raised by depressed mothers to see that lack of positive emotion leads to children who are depressed and anxious and are likely to stay that way through life. So while trust is important, so is *emotional availability.*

In the adult, emotional availability is a critical concept because it seems a stumbling block in so many relationships. Emotional availability means listening with your heart as well as your head. It means expressing feelings rather than just words. It means sharing emotional experiences not just the same room or even the same bed.

We have already seen the gender differences in both the processing and expression of emotion and these frequently lead to the perception that the male partner is emotionally unavailable to his partner. Some are genuinely unavailable - some just seem that way. Because expression is different does not mean, necessarily, that he is unavailable.

Someone is emotionally unavailable when they..

⇒ Listen to their partner while watching television

⇒ Listen to their partner while mentally rehearsing their golf swing

⇒ Report only the facts rather than feelings about a significant life-event

⇒ Send someone else to bring their partner home from the hospital

⇒ Forget their partner's birthday or anniversary

⇒ Don't know their partner's five most important dreams

Someone is emotionally available when they..

⇒ Encourage their partner to strive for their desired goals

⇒ Are present at all the tough times

⇒ Drop all other activities when their partner is in desperate need

⇒ Know their partner's worst fears

⇒ Validate their partner's expression of feelings and opinions

If there is trust, a mutual meeting of needs and emotional availability, you have a strong and secure attachment. When you are secure in your relationship you have the tremendous freedom to develop your individuality. You have this because…

1. Your needs are met

2. You are accepted for who you are

3. You have emotional support

4. Your energy is not being tied up in trying to resolve insecurity

As every fortunate child knows, security allows you to step out into the world with confidence in the safe knowledge that you have a loving and supportive family to catch you in the event that you fall. That same loving and supportive family also show a genuine interest in your endeavors, encourage you and provide the opportunity for you to share your experiences. Sharing experiences is important in learning. Sharing not only gives the activity a positive emotional association but also teaches more about the activity itself. For example, each time I give a seminar I learn a little more about the subject simply in the process of communicating the idea and getting feedback. For these reasons, secure attachment is the precursor of nurturing. It should be no surprise, therefore, that the evidence shows that securely attached children have higher IQ's.[41]

Similarly, a good adult relationship allows the freedom for each partner to develop themselves in being the best they can be. Such nurturing is an essential step in the development of a healthy relationship.

Of course, there is a difference between a child-parent attachment and an adult-adult attachment. A child knows that its parents are its parents and it is difficult for them, if not impossible, to change that status. Parents may be hostile, rejecting, and hurtful but for better or worse, they will always be the parents. This affords some security. Wives and husbands, on the other hand, can get divorced and

---

[41] van Ijzendoorn MH, van Vliet-Visser S. The relationship between quality of attachment in infancy and IQ in kindergarten. Journal of Genetic Psychology 1988 Mar;149(1):23-28

change their status. The possibility of this physical abandonment can create more doubt in the adult-to-adult relationship. If you want to have an outstanding relationship and if you want someone to really love you, you give them freedom. *A caged animal is a dependent animal.*

Some attachments are strong but they are not very secure. There are people who define themselves solely by their relationship with their partner. The relationship therefore becomes all-consuming and very little exists outside of it. When identity is invested in one relationship, the relationship becomes all-important. Often such people will hang on to their partners like extra strength velcro and their dependency controls the relationship. They are terrified of being abandoned and thus seek to control the relationship at all costs.

You know you are dependent when…

You don't have your own bank account

Your partner buys all your clothes

You always do what your partner wants to do

You feel unsettled if your partner is not with you

When I was growing up there were two neighbors who had dogs. On one side of our house lived a man with a German Shepherd named Traz. Each day the neighbor would march the dog down the street on a very tight leash. If Traz deviated from the man's expectations he would yell at the dog and sometimes hit it with a strap. The dog was never off the leash. Even when it was in the confines of its owner's back yard, Traz was still tied to a tree.

On the other side of the street, the neighbor had a Golden Retriever named Kringle. The man would walk the dog without leash under voice control. The dog would playfully run the sidewalk and it was always in the front yard, happily greeting people as they passed and occasionally jumping the fence to say hello to a passing friend. But whenever Kringle went off on a little adventure she would always return, tail held high.

One day, somehow Traz managed to escape the clutches of her owner. Despite endless requests, notices and rewards the dog never returned. Some said she had gone back to the wild.

Nurturing and Time

Time is perhaps our most important resource. We all get twenty-fours a day, seven days a week. How that time is spent is a critical relationship issue. Couples need to spend quality time together. They also need to spend quality time away from each other. The advantages of this are...

- Each party has the freedom that an independent life bestows

- When they get back together they have interesting new adventures to relate thus maintaining some novelty

- They are less likely to get bored

- They are more likely to appreciate each other

Although it is important for couples to have mutual goals, aspirations and values they don't need to have completely compatible leisure interests. Obviously, they do not want to have nothing in common but the research is quite clear on this point. The evidence strongly suggests that leisure compatibility is not related to marital satisfaction. In short, you don't need to do everything together to have a successful relationship. A loving relationship not only allows each partner to pursue independent goals, it can provide the catalyst for removing neurotic barriers.

Louise was a dependent woman who married young to a controlling man. When he left her in her mid-thirties with three children, she was absolutely frantic. Unschooled in the ways of the world, her first reaction was to latch on to the first man who would have her. Indeed, she was soon engaged to be married again, to another controlling individual who would feed off her dependency.

One afternoon while driving to the store with her two daughters, Louise got a flat tire. As Louise fumbled around, bemoaning her luck and panicking, her ten year-old daughter went to the trunk, hauled out the jack and proceeded to remove the damaged wheel. When her mother protested about this her daughter shot back, "Don't you hate being helpless?" The words reverberated around Louise's mind like a pinball on caffeine even as a kind passing motorist stopped to help restore the car's mobility. The wheel had fallen off her personal wagon and Louise was about to put it back on.

Within a few days she had called off her engagement. With her ambition matched by only by her anxiety, Louise started the difficult task of developing her independence, a stage that had been sadly avoided in childhood courtesy of overprotective parents. It was a painful process but slowly she learned to do things for herself. As is common with such a conversion, some of Louise's behavior swung too far the other way. She eschewed the company of men expressing no desire to remarry, or even date. She struggled to learn her independence.

Two years later she met Jack, a divorced accountant with two grown children. They started a friendship by sharing their interest in art. At tax time, Louise felt bold enough to ask Jack's accounting advice. Rather than doing the work for her, Jack showed Louise how to organize her books, finances and tax preparation. Two more years passed and their relationship developed. Jack encouraged Louise to return to school to finish her college degree, which she duly did. Jack also encouraged her to develop friends and take time for herself. When Jack finally asked Louise to marry her, he had one request - that she leave her job at a local manufacturing plant to pursue the career she had a special aptitude for - special education. Louise put that career move on hold for three more years, until her children had left home to begin their college careers. Then, in her early forties, secure in Jacks' love and armed with his support she courageously continued the retooling of her life by starting her career as a special needs teacher.

Apart from Jack's complete nurturing Louise had another great advantage. She knew about special needs education. She was deaf.

Nurturing Exercises

Here are some simple exercises to encourage your own ability to nurture.

- Write down your partner's goals and aspirations. If you do not know them ask her/him what they are.

- Devise three ways that you could help in the realization of those goals.

- Determine to arrange for each partner to have at least one night a week spent out with other friends or doing separate activities.

Step Eight

Romancing

As you learned in the early part of this book, romance is fired by the Novel Erotic Attachment, that distinctive and heady phase at the beginning of your relationship. You have already learned, and probably experienced, the fact that the NEA fades after a short time to be replaced by other more practical considerations. But just because the NEA fades over time does not mean that romance is likewise consigned to a few photos in your special album. Romance needs to be kept alive. You must keep contact with the special feelings that you have about each other and the relationship.

It is all too easy in the mayhem of everyday life not to make time for the romantic interlude. Whereas in the heady stages of the NEA, romance was natural and an essential priority, as the relationship matures you have to go out of your way to make sure that romance occurs at all.

The Essence of Romance

If you consider the days of the NEA and romantic love, you can see the elements that make up a romantic encounter.

Isolation. You could be in the center of New York but when you are in love, there are only the two of you. Romance excludes other people or intrusions.

You can create this sense of isolation by ensuring that you have no distractions. You might also go to places that are not bustling with people, have no neon intrusions and limited activities. [42]

You want the minimum intrusion because one of the features of romance is the exclusive attention you pay to each other.

---

[42] Admittedly, this might drive some couples bananas, but you get the idea.

> **10 things not to take with you on a romantic interlude.**
>
> **Children**
> **In-laws**
> **Friends**
> **Laptops**
> **Cell phones**
> **Pets**
> **Work**
> **Two cars**
> **Portable television**
> **Electronic games**

Attention. It's one thing to send the children off to their grandparents, fly to Florida, board the cruise ship but it's not a romantic interlude if he then spends all his time in the casino and she becomes irremovably attached to the spa. Romance, is above all, about making your partner feel special and you can only do that by *paying him or her some attention.*

> **Just being in a romantic place is not the same as being romantic**

Place. Although it is possible to share a romantic moment almost anywhere, location and setting are important in creating the right atmosphere and associations. It is frankly tough, for example, to be romantic in the utility room, surrounded by dirty washing, garbage and cat litter. For one thing, these objects are associated with drudgery and feelings that are virtually the complete opposite of those you are trying to engender.

Many people when asked to imagine a romantic spot, think of an uncrowded beach, with golden sand, deep blue water and gently swaying palm trees. The reason for this is that these stimuli are associated with complete relaxation, are not part of everyday experience and thus not associated with everyday routines and chores.[43] Moreover, this beach image is replete with sensual stimuli. You can almost feel the warm sand under your feet, hear the waves gently lapping to the shore, smell the sun tan lotion, and taste the Pina Colada. So, wherever the place you choose to go, ensure that it will enable you to spend time paying special attention to each other and has the right associations.

Memories. As I describe on page 167, experience is filed in the cells in your nervous system. These cells contain information about the sensory and emotional dimensions of the experience. These associations can be hooked and brought back into consciousness when one of these stimuli is re-experienced. For example, you will re-experience the romantic feelings of your honeymoon when you hear music that was played at the time. You can use this fundamental principle of human physiology to rekindle some of the romantic feelings in a number of ways.

First, your choice of location and activities for your romantic getaway should resemble places and activities associated with your initial courtship and the excitement of the NEA. This does not mean, of course, that you always have to go back to the town were you started dating. The town itself may have all sorts of other associations that run counter to the romantic feelings you are trying to recreate. There may be, however, certain places like a special restaurant or a specific hotel, that will have romantic meaning for you. You don't always have to return to the exact same place to resurrect the proper associations. For example, eating at an Indian (or any other ethnic) restaurant may have special significance to you. Perhaps that is where you finally agreed to get married. That Indian restaurant will have special significance that probably will have generalized to Indian restaurants. Visiting such a restaurant will likely create a nostalgic effect.

You can use the mechanism of memory and association in other ways. Not only can you try to make the connection between this trip and the early stages of courtship and the NEA, you can make any

---

[43] If your job was to clear the trash off an exotic beach your vision of a romantic spot might be quite different

romantic interlude more memorable if you mark its special nature with definite symbols. For example, if you enjoy a particularly romantic meal, you might keep the flowers from the table or matchbook from the restaurant as a symbolic reminder. Remember that the more special the object, the more suitable and powerful it is as a symbol. Keeping a copy of your bill and your credit card receipt from the restaurant is unlikely to have the same impact!

In this regard, my wife has introduced a particularly good family tradition. She buys Christmas ornaments whenever we go on a special trips. Each year, as we dress the Christmas tree, we can nostalgically revisit all of our special trips, not only in the past year, but in the years before that.

Everyday Romance
Planning romantic getaways is important but in today's hectic lifestyles such trips might not happen very frequently. You can't wait to be romantic once a year.

You can use the same principles of isolation, attention and association described above to keep the romance alive on a regular basis. The keys here are making your partner feel special by paying them attention and ensuring that you do joint activities without outside distractions.

As we all know, it is very easy to take your partner for granted so it is essential you step outside of this mode and on a regular basis attend to the romantic aspect of your partnership.

Here are some simple ways to show you care and that your partner is special.

Surprise gifts or trips

Thank-you notes

Flowers (even for men)

Dates (without the children)

Weekend trips/outings

Playing together

Taking over chores

Giving your partner time for themselves

Gift certificates (e.g. The masseuse, the mall, the beauty parlor, the golf course)

When Giving is a Problem
Giving is not just about writing a check. To be really good at giving you have to be really good at communicating. To come up with an appreciated gift you have to listen to your partner and know what would be meaningful to them. Several times in my career I have come across people who have given expensive gifts to their partner only to find their partner appreciative but disappointed. Their partners can recognize that these gifts are special but would have rather settled for something they really wanted - often for a fraction of the price. The meaning of giving a gift that is not at or near the top of your loved one's list is that you have not been listening - that you really do not know what it is that they want. This is compounded when you have given an expensive gift and shown that cost is not an issue.

Worse than giving a gift that you think your partner wants is to give a gift that you want. Giving your mate a new television for the bedroom because you want one is a little transparent and is not likely to endear you to your partner.[44]

Acting Together
Regardless of the pace and style of your lives, it is essential that you do some activities together. For one thing, separate lives lead to separate bedrooms. I once counseled a copy whose intimacy had been completely lost much to the chagrin of the husband. As I heard the story of their life unfold it was obvious that they did nothing

---

[44] Warning: A television in your bedroom can be harmful to you sex life

together. You cannot possibly expect to resurrect intimacy if sex is the only activity you plan to do together. Togetherness is a precursor for satisfying sex. In that regard, any activity that you do together is a stepping stone to greater intimacy. Cleaning the yard, doing the grocery shopping and even cleaning the dishes *together* are all preludes to greater intimacy.

> **Without special attention and time together alone, intimacy will disappear.**

Romance and intimacy go hand in hand. It is easy to slip out of romantic ways when overwhelmed by the obligations of everyday life. Many couples get mired in the stress of the rat race, are exhausted and co-exist as partners in the tasks of daily living. They completely lose touch with the romance and magic of their relationship. If you lose the feeling of being special, if you lose mutual attentiveness, sex will become an obligation. When sex becomes an obligation, intimacy dissolves in boredom.

The Role of Sex

Sex is a powerful force in any relationship. It has tremendous power which can both unite or destroy a couple. Sex, if properly consummated, can be the catalyst for loving actions. Mutually rewarding sex can unite a couple, substantially strengthening their attachment. As I highlighted in the first part of this book, the erotic component of the Novel Erotic Attachment is not itself love but by eliciting positive feelings and bringing the partners closer together, acts as a catalyst for love and the loving behaviors outlined in this book.

Sex is also a bargaining chip and a currency of control. There are gender differences in sex drive, particularly as the relationship develops. As we age, the hormones that drive female sexuality decline, whereas those that drive male sexuality do not. As a result, men tend to be more sexually interested than women as they age.

Sex often has a different meaning for men and women. For a man, sex is a physical drive - for women it is more psychological. Men's reproductive system continues functioning throughout their life.⁴⁵ As a result men, in general, are interested in satisfying their physical need whereas women have a special interest in the psychological aspect - of being attended to and nurtured. This leads to the reality of the common caricature of the man satisfying himself in a few minutes while the women feels used and gets nothing out of the encounter except considerable frustration and anger.

Because of its importance, sex becomes a currency of control in most relationships. Frequently his can lead to an ill-advised relationship between sexual arousal and anger.

In one case, one client's sexual advances were increasingly rebuffed by his girlfriend. He found that whenever he was getting sexually aroused he was also getting tense and aggressive. He was learning to associate arousal and anger - an association that frequently underpins crimes of sexual violence. Eventually he stopped approaching her altogether and this ultimately led to the break-up of the relationship.

Many people bring substantial baggage into the bedroom with them. The frequency of sexual abuse, especially but not exclusively among young girls, means that many women approach intimacy with anxiety, defensiveness and anger. It is difficult for them to address these issues with their mates for several reasons.

If the abuse was traumatic and especially if it occurred at a young age, the woman may not be consciously aware of the trauma. Frequently, such women only have a great sense of unease about sex but don't really know why. Often, they cannot remember large chunks of their childhood. This amnesia and unexplained anxiety can be a clue to childhood abuse.

In cases where there is conscious awareness of some abuse, there are frequently tremendous feelings of guilt and shame. Children and teenagers do not have the maturity, wisdom or experience to be able to put abuse into perspective. They will believe that they are in

---

⁴⁵ Women are born with 300,000 ova. Men make billions of sperm throughout their life span. During ejaculation, about 250 million sperm are released.

some way responsible for the abuse. Apart from their inherent inability to put this in a proper context, abusers typically tell their victims that they are to blame for the abuse.

The experience of abuse can generate tremendous anxiety and pain. Often, the experience is frightening and physically painful. In addition, perpetrators of abuse frequently make violent threats against the victim to keep them from talking. These are typically death threats against the victim or the victim's loved ones.

Sexual abuse is also very confusing to the victim. If the abuse is perpetrated by a family member like father or grandfather, the emotional confusion is enormous and the threat to the child's sanity severe. To be abused by someone on whom you depend is the most frightening kind of terrorism. It demolishes trust.

Sexual abuse is also confusing because it can produce pleasurable sensations in the most abhorrent of situations. The body is designed to react with pleasure to certain sorts of stimulation and this can happen even in a abusive situation. This leaves the victim feeling betrayed by her body and frequently leads to self-disgust and hate. Many women who have been sexually abused are substantially overweight and have body image distortions. A minority become anorexic. It is estimated that about 30% of women with a diagnosed eating disorder have experienced sexual abuse.

Joan consulted me when her frigidity was creating major marital problems. She had always been tense about sex and frequently needed a shot of alcohol to release enough tension to be able to be sexually active. It transpired that she had been sexually abused by her step-father - more frequently than she had previously remembered. She became uncomfortable when she even began to think about this problem and had basically lived her life avoiding the issue. This typically led to her tensing up when her husband approached her and ending with her exploding at her husband - clearly displaced anger against her abuser. Joan could not talk to her husband about these half-remembered matters out of tremendous guilt and shame as well as anxiety.

Once Joan had, for the first time, really addressed the problem, the fog began to lift on her field of screams. Carefully, we recovered the memories and processed them. Step by step Joan went through the stages of anger, sadness and acceptance.

Fortunately, Joan had a loving and understanding husband, more sympathetic now that he knew that Joan's reaction had nothing to do with him. Slowly they began gentle intimate activities designed to stop short of intercourse and allow Joan to relax. Using a variety of strategies designed to refocus Joan's attention away from abuse and to create a new link between arousal and enjoyment, the couple were able to begin their intimate voyage together after ten years of marriage. Similar stories have surfaced many times in my practice.

You don't have to be a victim of abuse to have conflicted feelings and negative associations with sexual arousal. The first sexual experience is typically not one of unmitigated bliss for both genders. Confusion, self-consciousness, shame and guilt are the more common experiences.

Many men also have early experiences that create associations between sexual arousal and a variety of feelings, like anxiety, anger, and humiliation. Such associations clearly interfere with mature sexual development.

Seven Ways To Improve Your Sex Life

Here are seven suggestions for increasing intimacy that go beyond watching provocative material and address the psychology of intimacy.

Spend some time doing something together prior to initiating sexual behavior. I have already outlined why any activity done together is a pathway to better relations in the bedroom. Ensure that, at some part of the evening, you have spent at least a few minutes making yourself physically and emotionally available to your partner. You cannot expect your mate to be sexually available to you, if you have not been available to them.

Keep your pre-sex talk, upbeat and fun. Your conversation prior to sex will set the tone for your intimacy. You want to create an atmosphere of fun and relaxation, even adventure. You might, for example, daydream together about your next vacation, or some fun shared activity. The last thing you want to do is to talk about issues that create anxiety. One couple I counseled made the mistake of discussing their family problems (a problem child and an intractable parent) each night before going to bed. It was hardly surprising that going to bed with their anxieties ruined their intimacy. Amusing trivia about the day, new jokes, old stories - anything that is relaxing will set the right tone. Don't forget that sex is a sensual activity so talking about sensual experiences (e.g. a great meal, a terrific work-out, a good swim) will also create the right mood.

Resolve any lingering issues from the day. You don't have to be talking about your problems for them to be occupying your mind. While you cannot solve all the problems of the world, any issues that have surfaced during the day or are currently preoccupying you or your mate need to be resolved, if at all possible. If they cannot be resolved outright, at least have a plan of how to move forward so that these problems can be comfortably shelved until the following day.

Remove the television from the bedroom. Watching the television in bed can be a problem because it brings the whole world into your bed which should be just for the two of you. Moreover, television will limit your conversation and contact and, depending on what you have been watching, may set completely the wrong tone. Don't expect a woman who is totally disinterested in sports to suddenly get interested in you when you become amorous the moment SportsCenter is over.

Don't argue in bed. The bed should, ideally, be a symbol of relaxation, sensuality and fun. If you argue between the sheets the bed is now associated with tension and disagreement. Anger and intimacy are not good bedfellows. Similarly, bed should not be a place where you do work even if your laptop does allow you to do the corporate accounts while propped up by two comfortable pillows.

Be physically comfortable. Sex is the ultimate physical experience and it requires physical comfort for maximum enjoyment. If you eat late, you stomach might feel full thus creating discomfort. If you have been drinking coffee or caffeinated drinks all night, your bladder might be the part of your anatomy that dictates the night's events. Making yourself as physically comfortable as possible, by taking a bath, for example, will increase your enjoyment.

A relationship without intimacy and romance becomes a coalition of roommates. Romance and sex are necessary to maintain the special contact and bond that a loving relationship has to offer.

Step Nine

Forgiving

It is inevitable that in the course of your most intimate relationship, conflicts and major disagreements will occur. One of the secrets of a successful relationship is ensuring that these muddy waters of disenchantment and anger don't harden into bricks of resentment.

Two of life's truisms that are particularly difficult to accept continually recur in our special relationships.

- You cannot control another person unless they let you
- Sometimes you have to give up dreams

Unless you come to terms with these truisms you are going to have a rough time in any close relationship.

Forgiveness is an act of selfishness. Smart selfishness but self-serving none the less. Consider the case of Marlene and Jeff, a middle aged couple with teenage daughters I saw after they had been married for twenty years.

Ten years prior to consulting with me, Jeff, then in his early forties, had left a secure corporate job to start his own consulting business. As is often the case, it took Jeff much longer than he had anticipated to establish a viable business that would support their previous lifestyle. In the meantime, the couple had used up almost all of their assets and, while not completely ruined, they had experienced a precipitous drop in their standard of living.

Marlene was furious. She felt she had been betrayed by Jeff. She thought he had been irresponsible and to blame for what she considered to be a humiliation. The decision to start an independent business had been one that Marlene had initially supported. Jeff had been honest with her about financial issues. This was definitely not one of those cases where the husband starts his own business and suddenly the wife discovers that he is used all their assets and they are all but bankrupt. Nonetheless, Marlene was angry and hurt.

It did not take too long before their physical contact dwindled to a distant memory. Jeff worked longer and longer hours, ostensibly out of necessity, but it also had the virtue of minimizing contact with his distressed wife.

Soon they were in separate bedrooms, living increasingly more distant lives. Jeff felt guilty. He certainly had not intended to damage the family. He hadn't set out to lose money. He had set out to give he and his wife the financial freedom he thought he could achieve.

Jeff was also mad. He felt that he was doing his best and that he was being punished. Both parties felt that they had been treated unfairly by the other. The stress and anger was in danger of ripping the whole family apart.

Gradually, Jeff had been able to get his business going and it started to generate a good income but Marlene was still miserable. A psychiatrist had prescribed anti-depressants and she had been on these, without too much improvement for four years. Feeling humiliated and ashamed about her lifestyle change she had cut herself off from friends and had a dismal social life. Their visit to me had been precipitated by a scare Marlene had got from suspicious results of a mammogram. Now Jeff had nearly given her cancer!

This scare with cancer was just what Marlene needed to let go of her fatal resentment.

Resentment is fatal. If you don't kill it, it will kill you

I explained to her that it was a good thing that her pre-cancerous cells had been detected because early detection was the best treatment. I mentioned to her that I had used some hypnosis to help people deal with cancer and if she thought it would be helpful I would be happy to spend a session with her teaching it to her. Still being in the initial panic phase over her possible diagnosis she agreed and I set up an individual session without Jeff present so I could demonstrate these techniques.

Marlene was a reasonably good hypnotic subject and seemed relaxed and receptive. I began by explaining that once something toxic got into your body it was very necessary to get rid of it immediately. Under hypnosis I told her the following.

"If toxic substances stayed in your body they would fester and poison your entire insides and would ultimately prove fatal. So as soon as a cancer had been detected, you have to immediately remove it. You don't ask questions. You don't try to understand why you have it, you don't waste your time blaming other people or circumstances that you believe may have contributed to the problem - you just do anything you can to remove it as quickly as possible. Fortunately, Marlene, you still have the power to get rid of this poison before it does you any more damage. Life is too short to wonder about the whys and wherefores - you must take swift action. When you exorcise this poison, you will feel so much better. You will be choosing life over death, you will be taking back the power in your life.

"Sometimes bad things like this just happen. It's nobody's fault. It might seem as if you should be able to blame someone for the poison but often it is not anybody's fault. Your job is to make sure that the poison doesn't kill you.

"You have the power to rid all damaging material from your mind and body. You can no longer let toxic substances control your life."

I then described a number of visual images of Marlene's cells attacking and killing any "life-threatening and destructive foreign particles."

At the next joint session, Marlene seemed much calmer. She was relieved that further tests had revealed no signs of malignancy. The whole experience had made her "realize how short life is" and how much she wanted to restore her relationship with Jeff who had been so supportive during her cancer scare.

Once Marlene had dropped her resentment, she and Jeff were able over time to work through their anger and frustrations and substantially improve their relationship.[46]

Marlene lost ten years of her life to resentment. Anger and bitterness will erode your body and I have seen several clients whose illness has been a direct result of the inability to give up frustrations.

This is not to say that Marlene was unjustified in her feelings about Jeff and the situation that resulted from his actions. Of course, she is going to be hurt and angry. It is not that those are unreasonable feelings or opinions. It is just that holding on to them for a long time is NOT ADAPTIVE. This is not a case of moral judgment, it is not a case of right or wrong or even a matter of degree it is about what is *most healthy and in the best interests of the person.*

This is why forgiveness is as much an act of self-preservation as it is of altruism. Through the years of Marlene's bitterness, she was the one suffering hourly with tension, depression and despair. Jeff suffered some of the consequences of Marlene's pain, but because it was not his, he could escape ninety-five per cent of the time.

> **No matter how unfairly you have been treated, the bitterness, anger and resentment are yours. You own it until you decide to get rid of it.**

This does not mean to say that you should dismiss anger and resentment. Obviously, important issues need to be discussed and aired but you cannot hang on to the negative feelings for too long. I have seen too many couples where such resentment has become fossilized and is irremovably embedded in the bedrock of the relationship.

It is important to make the distinction between acceptance and forgiveness. Marlene did not accept Jeff's behavior. She made it clear

---

[46] Please note that it was Marlene who did the hard work of dropping her resentment. Hypnosis is merely a tool, not a therapy and not magic. In this case, I believe that the hypnosis simply helped Marlene remove the barrier to the forgiveness that she genuinely sought.

that she did not want to be put in that position again. She was adamant that she would not support decisions that put them at so much risk. She also recognized her own responsibility in not being more informed before agreeing to the venture. In the end, after a decade, Marlene was able to say "I do not accept or endorse what happened. I am ready, however, to put it behind us and move on." Such sentiment is the root of the oft used edict, "I'll forgive but I'll never forget."

In the case above, forgiveness was made easier by the following factors.

Jeff accepted responsibility for his behavior. He had made every effort to understand and support his wife. In fact, he shared many of her same frustrations.

Jeff's behavior had not been malicious. He had not set out to specifically hurt his wife. On the contrary, he had set out to help her realize her dreams and provide more security for the entire family. Jeff could be accused of inexperience and excessive optimism but not malice.

The offending behavior and situation had largely been resolved. Jeff's business was doing well and they were making a financial recovery. It is going to be difficult to practice forgiveness if the offending behavior and situation continue. It would be very difficult for Marlene to forgive Jeff if he irresponsibly drained the family's finances year after year with no sign of progress. If hurtful behavior continues, forgiveness is an act of self-flagellation not self-preservation.

Marlene wanted genuinely to forgive but was blocked by her anger. In some situations, a hurt party simply does not want to forgive.

Some people are better at letting go than others. We all have our limits. There are some hurts and injustices that we could never forgive. Then there are those who cannot forgive anything or anyone. Their egos won't allow them to let go of grievances.

Learning How To Let Go

Several years ago, when I was living in England, an old college friend of mine called to seek my advice on a problem he was having with his fiance. Dave was a good guy who had gone on from college to become a pharmacist. Somewhat introspective by nature, he was one of those people whom it takes time to really appreciate. Now, in his early thirties, he had finally met the girl of his dreams and they were to be married. The dreams threatened to turn into nightmares, however, when Jill, his fiance, admitted to him that recently she had had a one night fling with an old boyfriend.

Jill was apologetic. She had regretted the incident the moment it happened. She had had too much to drink. She was absolutely clear that she loved Dave and wanted to spend the rest of his life with him - if he would still have her.

In long talks over the telephone Dave was able to understand that forgiving Jill was not condoning her behavior. And Dave still had a lot of trust in Jill. He just was not sure he could ever forgive her. One evening, Dave called saying he was coming into London over the weekend and he would like to meet me and talk so more.

"It will be great to see you again, Dave," I said, "but one thing. We are not going to talk about you and Jill." He muttered something about needing a break from thinking about that. "One last thing," I said, "You must do exactly what I ask."

I met Dave at Euston station around late morning. He was showing the signs of the stress that had been his constant companion for the past few weeks. After our exchange of hellos, we decided that this would be a good time to go and get lunch. In college we had both been Indian food junkies.

"I know this great Indian restaurant," I said. Dave and I started to reminisce about our favorite Indian dishes and we were positively salivating at the prospect of upcoming lunch. Well, Dave was but I was not. I knew we were not going there.

We walked on another half mile and I suddenly turned into a Middle east restaurant, which I knew was low down on Dave's list of favorite place to dine. At first, Dave was confused. "Hey, you've got the wrong restaurant," he said.

"No, I haven't," I replied.

"You said we were going to an Indian restaurant," he complained.

"No, I didn't," I replied. "I said I <u>know</u> of a good Indian restaurant. I didn't say we were <u>going</u> to one. We are going to this one."

"You know I don't like this sort of food," Dave complained but before his remonstration got out of hand I stopped him by saying "I told you I would spend the day with you provided you agreed to go along with exactly what I said."

Dave reluctantly, and somewhat huffily, took his seat at the small table by the window to which we had been led.

"Bastard," he muttered in my direction after the waiter had delivered some hummus to the table.

"Let it go, Dave. Let it go, now or else it's going to ruin our day," I insisted. It probably took Dave about fifteen minutes to calm down and to his eternal credit he even made a great effort to enjoy his lunch.

Things perked up a little for Dave after lunch. We found an arcade where they had a great table soccer machine. In college we had been inseparable table soccer buddies for two years and so we spent some time revisiting our skills. After that, we progressed to Regent's Park where I told him I had to make a stop at the University to collect some papers. When we got to the college, I parked him by the television in the students' lounge and disappeared. "I'll just be a few minutes," I said as I left him sitting solitarily on a well-worn sofa.

After an hour, I returned. Dave was really mad.

'What the hell, have you been doing?" he yelled in a rhetorical and overt display of temper that was untypical for Dave.

"I am so sorry, Dave," I said. "You have every right to be mad. It's a long story and I really apologize."

"I don't accept your apology," he said defiantly.

"Dave, you can carry on being mad, if you want. I am not going to be. I am going to enjoy myself but if you want to steam and sulk that's up to you."

I could see Dave taking a big sigh. He was making a big effort to let his anger go.

"Come on, " I said, "If we hurry we can get to Highbury and catch the Arsenal game."[47]

"I know what you've been doing," Dave said, as we hurried back to Euston station. "You've been testing me."

"I have?" I replied innocently. "What exactly have I been doing?"

"Getting me angry then making me drop it," he said.

"Just wanted to see if you could do it. Whether you could choose to disconnect your emotion from an idea."

"I nearly hit you," he said.

"There's plenty of time left, yet" I said. There was something about Dave that bought the wiseacre out of me.

"No more tests, okay," Dave said, rather firmly.

---

[47] Arsenal are one of London's premier soccer teams.

"Fine, but you see what you have to do. I know you still love Jill and want to marry her. You just have to disconnect the emotion."

I promised Dave no more tests but I could not resist one more opportunity to make a point when it arose naturally and serendipitously.

The soccer game was exciting and it was tied entering the last five minutes. With the game almost over, one of the Arsenal strikers had a chance to win the game but missed an easy opportunity to score. The crowd groaned.

"They'll never forgive him for that," Dave said.

"Yes, forty thousand people will never forgive him. The guy's only human. Most of them would do the same thing in his place. Come on, let's go, the game's over."

We got back to Euston station just in time for him to catch the train back north.

"It's okay. I think I'll make my connection," he said.

"To heck with that," I said "Just ensure you make the disconnection."

I don't know whether my games that day had any influence on my good friend. He and Jill have been happily married for fifteen years.

To forgive you have to disconnect the hurt and the emotion from the idea of violation. Some people are better able to disconnect the emotion than others.

How To Disconnect The Emotion

Some people are incapable of letting emotion go. They harbor resentments over every slight and their anger never seems to fade. These, typically, are people who have an enormous core of anger that erupts volcanically. Under the slightest provocation they spew out a pyroclastic cloud of magma that showers down on anyone and anything that has the misfortune of being in the way. These people are seismically unstable and their ability to forgive is a serious fault.

All emotions are the result of social perceptions. The anticipation of an unpleasant experience creates anxiety, the violation of personal values creates guilt and the perception of being treated unfairly creates anger. When you feel you have been wronged you are going to feel anger. Dissipating the anger so that you can disconnect it from the concept of whatever is bothering you can be done by several means.

Discussing the situation and letting the other party know how you feel is important. Anger, appropriately vented, is an act of self-expression.

There are various ways of venting anger healthily.

- Use visualizations to dissipate anger. Using imagery to help reduce emotion is very useful.[48]

- Physical activities (especially exercise) not only decrease the tension associated with anger but can be satisfying psychologically. It is an adaptive way of expressing our natural fight reactions that occur when we have been violated.

- Writing down feelings should ensure that they are not stuffed inside and left to fester. Don't worry about punctuation, style or even spelling. Its an exercise in letting the emotion flow down your arm and out through your pen. It does not have to be in letter format. If you intend to send a letter, don't send your first draft and wait for at least forty-eight hours before letting it fly. Variations on this theme include talking into a tape recorder.

---

[48] There are some visualizations to reduce anger and frustration in my book *7 Steps To Wellness* (Stepwise, 1998)

- Talking your feelings out with an independent third party who is a good listener is also a great strategy. Make sure that the listener is a listener - you don't need a problem-solver at this point - merely some ears and encouragement to let the words flow. A problem solver is likely to inhibit your flow of emotion and be counterproductive at this stage. In most cases there is not too much need for a problem-solver - either you are going to be able to disconnect the emotion or you're not.

Once your anger is out and processed you are in a position to give it up if you so choose.

Ways of Putting the Hurt Into Perspective

Disconnecting the emotion is the critical action in forgiveness but reframing your perceptions about the violating event will help minimize the emotion, too. Remember anger comes from the perception that you have been treated unjustly. If you could restructure your perceptions so that the injustice seems less severe, the intensity of the anger should be reduced.

There are many books that take the concept of "cognitive restructuring" and apply it to different life-problems - depression, anxiety, relationships. In the context of forgiveness, cognitive restructuring means seeing the affront in a less hurtful light. Ways of doing this include..

- Remembering a similar occasion some years ago. Think about how you reaction has changed over time. Consider what happened or what you did to make the hurt go away. Is that action appropriate in this case?

- Project forward to determine how you might feel about this in three weeks time, in six months time, in five years time.

- Put yourself in the other person's situation. Can you understand why they took the action that offends you? Ask yourself..

⇒ Did they do it maliciously?

⇒ Would you have acted differently in their situation or might you have done the same thing?

The last question is crucial. It is easy for all of us to be critical about other people. It is more difficult to honestly ask ourselves how we would really behave in the same situation. Judge not lest ye be judged.

> **Don't criticize other people's footwear until you have had a chance to walk in it.**

In the final analysis, forgiveness is a question of whether you can disconnect the anger from your perception that you have been violated.

Step Ten

Understanding

Understanding is essential for effective behavior management. This is as true for intimate relationships as it is for any other aspect of life.

A Crash Course On Human Nature

The fundamental principles of human nature can be reduced down to some simple ideas.

Experience is encoded in the nervous system. It is filed away in the complex neurobiology of cells and carries with it sensory and emotional meaning. For example, suppose your initial experience of lilies was on a fun picnic on a beautiful summer's day with your family. This experience will be recorded deep in your nervous system. The visual and sensory complex of lilies will be associated with warm sunshine and good feelings about your family. This is part of your filed experience. Things that look like lilies will elicit some similar warm feelings.

Let's suppose you went on the same picnic, but as you went wading into the lilies for the first time you felt violently sick by the virtue of the fact that the chicken in your sandwich had not been fully cooked. Now lilies are associated with feelings of nausea and severe physical distress. Obviously, the meaning of lilies in these two examples is completely different. In one case lilies mean warmth, serenity, and love and in the other they mean nausea, queasiness and vomit.

All experience is encoded this way, according to meaning. This means that it is difficult, sometimes impossible, to revise the meaning a stimulus (like lilies) has simply by trying to reason you way out of it.

In the kingdom of human nature, experience is king. It does not matter that the meaning you attach to something does not make sense (lilies don't make people sick), it is very difficult to talk yourself out of experience. The primitive brain which houses emotion is not only older but has precedence over the more recently developed, neocortex which "houses" our logic centers. In short, emotion and meaning will override logic, especially where sense impressions and the emotion attached to them are strong.

You cannot wipe out experience. Strong experiences can only be modified by restructuring the meaning attached to them or by providing a new set of experiences that are different. In the example above, this would mean re-experiencing lilies in a more positive and pleasing way. Several critical points flow form this simple analysis.

Initial experiences are powerful because they become the foundations for your experience database. Initial experiences become established as the norm, the foundation on which all other experiences and behaviors are built. This is precisely why the first six years of life are critical. Within that time-frame, a child will have experienced many of the fundamentals of life - all of the emotions and many of the situations that dictate and determine interpersonal relationships, like trust, sharing, commitment, communication - in fact, virtually all of the *10 Steps* outlined in this book.

A lot of collective experience resides within us unconsciously. That experience can be hooked at any time by a stimulus (an event, a place, an action) that is similar. Suppose that you did have the association between lilies and nausea. The experience file on lilies could be opened when you encountered a stimulus with ..

..similar sensory qualities. For example you were browsing an art gallery and saw a painting of yellow flowers. You were in a perfume shop and smelled the scent of lilies.

..similar contextual qualities. For example, you read about an outbreak of food poisoning from ill-prepared chicken

..similar linguistic qualities. You met somebody called Lilly. It would be unfortunate if you felt nauseated on meeting a complete stranger simply because of such an association but that is the way the nervous system works!

In the example above, the stimuli is a simple one, lilies, and based largely on a single experience. Much more significant associations are created around more complex and frequently occurring contexts. Feeling queasy at the sight of lilies is one thing, feeling queasy when someone raises their voice, or tries to hug you or offers you a compliment is quite another.

This collective encoded experience is, in the vernacular, called your "baggage." Understanding your baggage and your partner's will go a long way to laying the foundations of a great relationship.

All of your experiences are stored in a great big filing cabinet called your unconscious. Occasionally, you open a drawer of that filing cabinet and consciously look at its contents. There are files that your consciousness does not want anything to do with, despite the fact that they contain important clues to your actions and your life.

How to Access Your Experience Filing Cabinet

Many of the associations that you have filed away in the recesses of your nervous system will be known to you even though their origin may be unclear. But your reactions to other important contexts and stimuli may not be so obvious.

As implied above, your conscious mind will want to avoid associations that involve discomforting, emotional experiences.

Therapists have devised all manner of tools to access your experience filing cabinet. To access your filing cabinet through your consciousness, therapists will simply ask you direct questions about your experience. For example, if you have a problem with intimacy they might ask you..

What exactly do you feel in an intimate situation?

What comes into your mind in an intimate situation?

What intimate experiences have you had?

Therapists have also devised ways of accessing your filing cabinet indirectly, bypassing conscious filters. Some techniques that have been used include..

Free Association. What *immediately* comes into your mind when presented with a particular stimulus?

Hypnosis. This allows the person to relax conscious filters

Dream Interpretation. Conscious safeguards are often down at night during sleep and even during day-dreaming. This allows some unconscious material to surface.

Linguistic analysis. The words and expressions people use and the stories they tell often have hidden meaning. This allows sensitive material to get past conscious filters and be detected and interpreted by an observant therapist.

Some time ago I was working with a depressed woman who was having difficulty in communicating and/or accepting the apparent powerless position she occupied within her marriage. No matter how much I tried to approach the subject at a conscious level, I could not get a response from her. So I started a conversation about her home. Before long she was telling me about a bird, her husband's pet, that lived in a cage in their living room. She told me that she frequently had an urge to release "the poor trapped animal and let it fly out of the window to freedom." I don't think she was talking just about the bird.

Now all this may be sounding to you too much like therapy and hard work. I am not about to suggest that you take a crash course in hypnosis and dream interpretation and start delving into your partner's unconscious. I do believe, however, that within limits of what is possible and reasonable, understanding each other's key experiences and associations is fantastically valuable.

Consider the following case of Mike and Justine who were a professional couple who sought my help for a number of problems in their marriage. One of Mike's major complaints was that Justine could be very rejecting and cold. She would occasionally go into long tirades against him, criticizing him for all manner of shortcomings, some of which were true, some of which were exaggerated and some of which had no basis in reality whatsoever.

When the three of us examined this more closely, we found out that Justine was particularly hostile when she believed Mike had not paid her enough attention, or had paid another woman more attention than she got. This was not always the case. There were some women that she did not care about, others clearly threatened her. This mixed picture had made it difficult for both of them to see that Justine felt insecure when Mike was around dark-haired, attractive (by Justine's standards) women. Further discussion revealed that Mike was doing nothing to justify Justine's insecurity. He wasn't flirting or encouraging these women at all and they were not aggressively pursuing him. This was Justine's *over-reaction* that had little to do with Mike's behavior. We subsequently discovered that Justine's father had broken up the family by eloping with a brunette. To Justine, brunettes meant infidelity and betrayal.

Once Mike understood that Justine's reaction was a response to a past event and not anything to do with him he was able to distance himself from his wife's criticism, become less defensive and attempt to adopt a more helpful posture. Once Justine recognized where the anger was coming from, she could begin to control it better. Between them they could adapt a new strategy for jointly managing the problem and move from a downward spiral of anger and recrimination to an updraft of mutual help and hope.

Many relationship difficulties begin when personal baggage is hurled at an unsuspecting partner. The partner then understandably counter-attacks and before long there's baggage flying everywhere. Often, when baggage flies it ends up at the wrong destination.

Compatibility

Couples are compatible in the sense that one partner's baggage does not trigger the other's. In the example mentioned above, Mike was not oversensitive to Justine's ungrounded suspicions of his fidelity. This enabled him to manage this situation with sensitivity rather than defensiveness. Imagine what would have happened, however, if Justine's criticisms had touched a raw nerve in Mike. The mix would have been explosive.

The most common difficulties in marriage occur when the partners' neuroticism and sensitivities feed into each other. Consider a case where he has a hang-up about sex and she is oversensitive to rejection. You can see that their bedroom is going to turn into a battle zone peppered with anger, frustration and ultimate withdrawal. Because both partners are emotionally charged about the issue it is going to be difficult for them to start managing the situation rationally.

> **Incompatibility occurs when the partners' neurotic needs conflict with each other.**

When the partner's neurotic needs don't conflict with each other, as in the case of Mike and Justine, there is a real opportunity for growth.

In his excellent book *Getting the Love You Want,* Harville Hendrix[49] takes the position that one of the main reasons for marriage is that it challenges us to extend ourselves and change in ways that we might not otherwise achieve if we were unmarried. I think it is true of all of our best relationships that they challenge us to develop. The biggest challenges to self-development within our most intimate relationships are to..

..help our partners moderate their sensitivities and neuroticism even as we are the target of their displaced and projected anger, frustration and anxiety

..have the courage to abandon our sensitivities and manage our emotions more effectively

---

[49] Harville Hendrix, Getting the Love You Want, HarperPerennial, New York, 1990

When couples are able to mutually moderate each other's neurotic needs they truly have a loving and successful relationship.

Exercises in Understanding

Based on the above explanation, here are some exercises that will help you understand and improve your compatibility quotient.

First, you need to access your experience filing cabinet and see what your responses are to some important relationship concepts.

In will be a helpful to get a pencil and notebook in which to write your answers.

In the first exercises, write down the first thing that comes into your head as you see each word. Note any emotions, images or ideas that might convey what these words actually mean to you.

Relationship

Men

Women

Trust

Anger

Intimacy

Sex

Childhood

Independence

Control

Conflict

Money

In-laws

Home

Parents

Sharing

Romance

Family

Friends

How did you do? There are several outcomes to this exercise.

1. The words triggered a cascade of thoughts and emotions. You could not stop writing. This is terrific! If these concepts elicited a strong response it is quite possible, even likely, that you experienced *conflicted feelings* and ideas. There is absolutely nothing wrong with that. Life is not simple and we often have very mixed emotions about the important things and people in our lives.

Mixed emotions are a sign of complexity and indicate that you have accessed meaningful feelings. By continuing to look inside your experience filing cabinet you will have a clearer understanding of your different responses and what they really mean.

2. The words generated a steady trickle of ideas. This is the probably the most typical response. Continued practice will help keep the trickle flowing. Remember, gold can be panned from the slowest flowing streams.

3. If you got absolutely no response at all from this exercise, try it this time with the television turned off! It may be that you were too distracted or not relaxed. In any event, these words are meaningful, emotional symbols. You are blocking.

In an ideal situation, you can get your partner to do the same exercise. If you are really adventurous, each partner can try to predict the others' responses. This is a terrific exercise for couples with advanced communication skills. It will open a discussion of the real issues in your relationship.

The Compatibility Grid

The above exercise may have given you some clues as to where your sensitivities and "hot buttons" are, if you did not know that already. If you have been with your partner for more than five years there is a good chance that he/she will be able to give an opinion as to what your sensitivities are.

The purpose of this exercise is to see how you and your partners, needs and hot buttons interact. As we have seen earlier, if they feed each other, sparks are going to fly.

For each partner write down the issues and/or situations that generate the most emotion.

For example, Justine in the case mentioned earlier, identified her problem as follows.

I get angry when Mike pays attention to other women.

Then for each situation write down what you think, feel and do in that situation.

In Justine's case

I think he is losing interest in me and that he is going to have an affair. I get really mad. I want to kill him. I yell at him and am really mean.

Now we need to see how your partner reacts to this situation.

In Justine's case, Mike typically reacted to her outburst with the following thoughts, feelings and behavior.

175

I don't know what's got into her. I hate her when she is like this. How can she not trust me? I give her everything. I am angry. I don't want anything to do with her.

In this dance, Justine's neurotic anxiety creates irrational behavior which angers Mike. He then withdraws which in Justine's mind *confirms her neurotic suspicions that he has lost interest in her.*

When people are neurotic they often provoke the very behavior they fear the most

What needs to happen now is to consider ways in which this dance can be changed and Mike and Justine's behavior be made more *adaptive.*

Obviously the answer to this is not to play into Justine's anxiety. It would be unreasonable, not to mention, inappropriate, if Mike allowed Justine to prevent him from talking to brunettes. It is not right that Justine's neuroticism control Mike's behavior. That is exactly, however, what happens in many cases. The neurotic person's behavior and emotion is so intense and persistent that it can overwhelm their partner's rationality. You don't want your relationship to turn into a game of "The One With the Most Neuroses Wins."

So my question to Justine was

What could Mike to do in this situation to make it more likely you will manage your fears?

Answers such as "spending all his time with me" or "not talking to other women" were not allowed. After some discussion it emerged that Justine would find it helpful to get some reassurance from her husband. Perhaps he could make sure that Justine was included in the conversation or kept physically close.

Mike was asked to come up with ways he could reassure his wife in these situations without forfeiting the right to have normal conversations with other women.

First, Mike reassured Justine that he had no intentions of being unfaithful - an idea she completely accepted when she was rational and not confronted by her worst fears. Mike agreed that he could, where possible, make more of an attempt to include Justine in these conversations and attempt to remain physically close to her. He also came up with the idea for a simple signal to Justine that he was thinking of her. For one of those romantically special reasons that couples share, the earlobe had a particular pride of place in their intimacy. In sensitive situations he would periodically touch his earlobe as a signal that he was aware of Justine and thinking about her.

Now to you, this may seem like the third base coach sending instructions to his baserunner but it worked as effectively as a Nolan Ryan fastball. Justine associated the gesture with playfulness and whenever she saw Mike do this, not only was she reassured that he was thinking of her but it elicited warm feelings of fun. that were incompatible with anxiety.

Obviously there are an infinite number of ways couples work to address each other's anxieties. It is working together to resolve these problems that is the crux of a great relationship. Incidentally, after a few weeks of Mike's signaling, and some therapy to resolve Justine's anger over her father, the necessity for earlobe touching faded.

Note that Mike and Justine were able to resolve this problem and strengthen their relationship because ..

- They were committed to the relationship

- Mike was able to understand and accept that Justine's anger was not really anything to do with him

- They were able to talk out their feelings and not let the anger simmer and turn into a grudge

- They did not let other issues intrude to confuse the issue

By understanding how your moods and sensitivities interact you can pinpoint the trouble spots in your relationships and, if you have the collective mind to do it, really enhance your partnership

More Exercises

Within a relationship each party leads independent and individual lives. Hopefully, these are meaningful lives that intersect with each other in a rewarding way. But they are separate and it's easy, in the course of busy lives, to lose contact with the substance of your partner's life. You might know how they spend their time but that is different from actually experiencing it. So, make the attempt to really understand your partner's experience by trying to experience it for yourself. There are two exercises that you could do to help you with this.

1) Role reversal. To understand more about your partner's life swap roles for a day or at least a few hours, if at all possible. You may think you know how your partner spends their working day but until you experience it for yourself, you won't ever understand it.

2) Observe. If it is not possible to actually switch roles, spend a typical day with each other. That way you will understand how your partner spends their time, typical daily pressures and experiences.

A relationship is a growing, active entity. The more you learn how to understand the relationship, the more you have learned how to improve it.

Getting Help

There will be times when even the best of relationships gets stuck. Disagreements, stress, over-commitment can all conspire to take the uniqueness out of the relationship and reduce it to a union of strangers.

Open hostility, traumatic life-events, transitions from one developmental stage of the relationship to another, can not only paralyze the partnership, it can sink it into a mire of despair.

Throughout this book, I have given you pointers on how you can help yourself into a better relationship. There are literally hundreds of other books all trying to do much the same thing. There comes a time, however, when no book or tape can solve the problem. As you have learnt from this book, some problems can be overcome with knowledge, new tools and skills. Sometimes, however, you need the reality of a new experience and the intervention of other people to help you see, feel, and act your way out of a difficult situation.

When To Seek Help

Ideally, a couple can resolve all of their problems and work out their differences without resorting to outside help. Reality, however, suggests that there will be times when seeking help will be useful if not essential. Here are the circumstances in which professional help is essential.[50]

When there is open hostility. Hostility is corrosive. It wears away the fabric of the relationship until nothing remains except a few charred strands. Moreover, hostility is personally damaging and no-one should have to tolerate it for a prolonged period.

Physical violence should not be tolerated. If you feel you are in danger of physical (including sexual) abuse, leave the situation.

---

[50] Essential, that is, if you are a rational human being trying to salvage your relationship.

| **You can't have a loving relationship if you don't feel safe** |

Verbal and emotional abuse are less immediately devastating but in the long run can be just as bad, or worse, than physical assaults. Bruises heal in a few days, self-esteem may never recover.

It is also easy to slip into a pattern of accepting abuse. Many of my clients have justified their abusive treatment. One client said to me that her mate only got really abusive about twice a month, as if this was somehow an acceptable frequency. After this I started to ask my clients about the frequency of hostile events to determine whether there was a frequency at which hostility became intolerable. The fact is, that very few people are hostile, mean and abusive *all the time.*

Everyone has their own limits and tolerance, of course, but my own completely unscientific and anecdotal research suggests that once the hostility and abuse occur more than 20% of the time,[51] even the most patient of partners seems to be moved to action.

In any event, abuse and hostility should not be allowed to continue unchecked. Once this level of hostility has been reached it is very unlikely you, as a couple, will be able to work it out for yourselves. Hence, professional help is a necessity in this situation.

When communication breaks down. As you have read in this book, communication is an essential part of a good relationship. If communication stops, the relationship sinks. Obviously, if you are not communicating there is no way of refloating the boat. A trained counselor is an ideal person to help analyze your communication difficulties and get you talking and listening to each other again.

When you there is a difference of opinion over a critical issue. You don't have to be in a personal or relationship crisis to cross the portals of the counselor's office. Frequently, there are differences of opinion over important life choices that could stand the input of a trained professional.

---

[51] This means that, on average, six days out of every month are characterized by hostility and tension.

A couple of whom I am particularly fond, disagreed over whether to extend their family. This couple are in their mid-forties, so they might have had to adopt if they chose to have more children. The wife wanted another child but her husband was really against the idea of extending the family. They already had one child and the debate hinged on the effect either having or not having another child might have on their only daughter. The mother had been an only child and was concerned that her daughter would grow up lonely, with a small immediate family and the burden of responsibility for her parents as they grew older. Her husband was not convinced that this was the case at all, pointing out there was no guarantee that a second child would fill the gaps in their daughter's life that the mother foresaw.

One evening they raised this issue in my company. It was clear where they both stood but because they have a loving relationship both were able to appreciate, if not endorse, the other's point of view. Both, I believe, would have given up their position, albeit reluctantly, if the other had completely insisted. The question really was quite a simple one. What impact does having (or not having) a second child have on the development and subsequent life experience of the first child. Not wanting to mix my social and professional capacities, I suggested that they make an appointment with a local clinical psychologist whom I knew to be an excellent practitioner.

They did make an appointment and by the time it was over, their dilemma had been resolved. The clinical psychologist, herself a mother of four, was emphatic that their child's experience of life would in no way be impaired if she did not have a sibling.[52] The wife was completely reassured by the therapist's sensitive handling of the issue. In fact, she felt considerable relief that she would not be depriving her daughter by having no more children. The dilemma was resolved and they have never looked back at the decision since.

Although this may seem an overly simple but none-the-less real life example, consider what would have happened if they had not sought professional advice. If they had drifted on and taken no action

---

[52] This is not always the case but I believe it was good advice given the life circumstances of this family

by default, the wife would have been resentful of her husband for "getting his way" and probably guilty for not meeting the needs of her child. If they had gone ahead and had another child there was a chance that the husband would have been resentful leading to an impaired relationship, not only with his wife, but also the new child. By being willing enough to listen to expert advice and loving enough to give up their position if it warranted, they were able to have someone else help them make their decision. It was not the counselor's decision not to pursue further children, it was the counselors expert input that *allowed them to make the decision with confidence and comfort.* A major life decision satisfactorily resolved for a $100 investment.

When there is a loss of intimacy. Physical intimacy can fade as quickly as the morning mist and when it does a critical piece of the relationship puzzle is lost. As we have already seen, sex is important because it cements attachment.

Intimacy can be lost for many reasons. Stress, overload, anger, declining sex drive, fatigue, depression, poor communication can all erode intimacy. Although many couples have a sexless relationship, this is rarely by mutual consent. This lack of intimacy not only loosens attachment but it also threatens to spread resentment. Counseling will help clarify the reasons for this loss of intimacy and help restore it, if that is what the couple wants.

When you are on the brink of doing something critical, like getting a divorce. There are defining moments in our lives when we take actions that have life-long ramifications for us and others around us. At these momentous times we are driven by strong emotions that make it difficult to see alternative courses of action. At these times it is worth the investment of even one session with a counselor. He or she might help restore your perspective or even endorse your decision-making. Remember, at times of high emotion we cannot reliably trust in our own judgment, especially where major decisions are concerned.

Ultimately, the counselor's job is not to save or rescue the relationship as much as they would like to be able to do so. Their job is to diagnose the problems of the relationship and offer tools to help make life more manageable. Sometimes, counseling cannot save a relationship. Occasionally, the exercise allows a smoother termination of the relationship. It can also provide insight which is important because many people are prone to carry their relationship issues from one union to the next. It is hardly surprising that the divorce rate is higher for second marriages than it is for first ones.

All of this presupposes that both parties are willing to seek help which is often not the case.

Seeking Help

A willingness to seek independent help is the sign of a healthy partner and a healthy relationship. Seeking help is not an admission of failure. Seeking help is a courageous recognition that there is a limit to self-analysis. Seeking help is a courageous recognition that there are perspectives other than your own. Seeking help is a courageous recognition that you are willing to abandon control over a particular issue.

Going to a counselor does not mean that you have insurmountable problems. You can use a therapist as a sounding board for issues that require more input from an independent source. I personally have used marital counseling myself for issues that were too important for my wife and I to resolve without listening to experienced, independent input. There are times when two people are too close and invested in the relationship to be able to see all the angles of an important issue.

Here are some pointers to consider when you summon the courage to seek help.

Get a trained counselor. There are many people parading as counselors who are not qualified to do so. Ask to see credentials. Any reputable counselor will be state licensed. Ask about their education and experience. What training have they received? How long have they been in practice? How long have they been working with couples?

Ask what type of therapy he or she practices. Ask him or her to describe the principles of such therapy. It is common for many practitioners to describe themselves as eclectic. This means they take from many different approaches and adapt them to suit the needs of the presenting couple. This is a very reasonable position, especially because many of the different schools of therapy overlap substantially and the differences between them are more apparent than real.

Ask about the counselor's training and experience. Training is necessary but not sufficient to ensure that this particular counselor is for you. A good counselor is able to apply technical competence creatively, adapting it to each situation and couple. A large part of a counselor's success depends on how they influence the partners. Their influence will be determined as much by their personality and style as by their technical competence.

Get referrals to help get you started. Personality, style and technical competence determine the counselor's success. As a result, one counselor might work very well for one couple but not at all with another. Because everyone's experience is different, a counselor who might have worked wonders for your friends may not work for you. Referrals from people you know are good starting points but not necessarily the best choice for you. Having said that, you need to be very careful of the next point.

Be as objective as possible. Most people will prefer counselors who tell them what they want to hear. Understandably, most people present themselves in the best light possible and want to be congratulated rather than confronted. This is especially true in relationship counseling where the relationship dynamics and issues get carried into the counselor's office. There is a difficult tightrope to walk here. You don't have to stay with a counselor who is not working out for you but neither do you want to walk away just because a therapist is telling you things you find uncomfortable.

Understand your counselor's strategy. Getting your counselor to explain his/her game-plan is one way to walk this tightrope successfully. One introductory session should be enough to tell you whether you are prepared to set up further sessions. At the end of that first session ask the counselor about his/her initial impressions and what course of action is recommended. Discuss a time-frame and what would be required from you both within and outside the sessions.

If you are satisfied with this approach, make a firm commitment to a limited number of sessions, typically four to six. You may well need more than this number of sessions but it makes for a reasonable initial commitment. Committing to this number also allows you to get to know how the counselor works and whether therapy is likely to be effective. Do not worry about formalizing such an arrangement. The reality is that if you do not feel happy with your counselor, you are going to walk away anyway. Give you and your counselor a chance by committing to a few sessions.

Ask about the policy of seeing partners individually. As I have already intimated elsewhere in this book, it is typical for partners entering couples' counseling to have a covert or overt desire to simply have their partners do all the work and make the necessary changes. The question frequently arises whether either of the partners needs individual therapy in addition to the relationship counseling and, if they do, who should conduct that therapy. I do not conduct individual therapy with clients I am also seeing together for several reasons.

If I see one partner for therapy it conveys the message that one person is in need of more help and thus I run the danger of colluding with the superiority complex of the other partner.

I also run the danger of the partner in therapy feeling that we have a 'special' relationship and that this is to his/her advantage in the couple's work. This might also alienate the non-therapy partner into feeling that they are the outsider in the couple's work. Overall, therefore, I do not believe seeing the same person for relationship and individual counseling is a very good idea.

By just confining my activities to the relationship I am also making a strong statement that the relationship is an entity, worthy of attention in its own right and more than just the sum of the two individuals.

This is not to say that individual therapy is not a good idea for those undergoing couple's counseling. It is often a very good idea. Often there is a need for both partners to have both individual and joint therapy. One arrangement that works well in this situation is to have each partner have their own therapist and then have the therapists work together as a team to conduct joint couple's counseling. If you are lucky enough to find therapists who work well together as a team and are experienced at doing conjoint therapy this can be very effective. Not only are the therapists informed about each partner's issues, they can together model how a successful partnership works. It is preferable, and most common, to have a male and female therapist, at least for male-female clients. The main drawback of this approach is the expense, because there are two therapists conducting the joint therapy and both will want to be paid their sessional rate.

Clarify the business end of the arrangement. Be clear about what the sessional charge is and ask how long a session lasts. What payment arrangements are expected? You want to clarify these business matters early on. You don't want them interfering with your relationship with the therapist at a critical point in your work together.

Ask about their policy of taking phone calls, faxes or any other form of communication, from one or other partner. Relationships are a constant struggle for attention and control. It is hardly surprising that these struggles are played out just as much with the relationship counselor as they are in virtually every other sphere of life. It is frequent, therefore, for partners to communicate with counselors independently, often behind the other partner's back. A therapist does not want to be in a position of colluding with one member of the couple, or keeping secrets that should be shared with the other partner.

Although it is wise to use an occasional session with a counselor as good preventive maintenance, most people turn to a counselor when their relationships are in turmoil. Not seeking help from a qualified expert when your union is in trouble is defensive and indefensible. If the wheels were coming off your car, you would presumably try to get them fixed. Of course, you might simply discard the car before even checking whether it could be repaired - a regrettably impulsive and costly approach that is often repeated when relationships break down.

Excuses, Excuses

Here are some of the major excuses for avoiding therapy and how to counter them.

Excuse #1: I don't need anyone to work out my problems. I can do that on my own.
Answer: You do need advice so you can clearly understand what's going on and to see your options. There is a limit to self-analysis.

Excuse #2: I don't need anyone to run my life
Answer: A therapist has no desire to control your life. They recognize that you will have to make your own decisions. They can make your decisions, *informed* decisions.

Excuse #3: I don't want anyone else to know about the details of our relationship. This should stay private.
Answer: Therapists are used to hearing about intimate details, many of which are far more troublesome than yours. Besides, all therapy is confidential.

Excuse #4: It's too expensive.
Answer: Compared to the cost of divorce, misery and stress, it's cheap.

Excuse #5: It won't do any good
Answer: How do you know until you try? Some of my biggest successes have been with people who started off very cynically. Besides, after you are divorced you don't want to be wondering whether you should have gone to seek help.

It is natural that the first time you see a therapist you will feel apprehensive, a little inhibited and even cynical. Hopefully, after the first session you will have appreciated the opportunity to talk to somebody who listens intently to you and makes every effort to understand your position. Clearly, trust needs to be developed on the basis of experience but even after your initial meeting you should feel that your therapist is somebody you can trust. If you cannot trust your counselor, find another one[53].

Who Makes The Decision To Seek Help?

Some couples are enlightened enough to mutually agree to seek help when their relationship gets stuck. More typically, however, one partner is anxious to seek help while the other resists the idea. This situation is typically resolved in the following ways.

1. The enthusiastic partner never can convince the resistant one to participate and so he (but more typically, she) goes on her own. This is an acceptable strategy. You cannot force your partner into therapy.

2. The enthusiastic partner presents some threat or ultimatum to the resistant one. This might get the resistant partner into therapy but they generally turn up with all the enthusiasm of depressed sloth. Someone press-ganged into counseling typically shows up to sabotage therapy, but at least you tried.

3. The resistant partner agrees to seek help but for some reason or another the appointment never quite gets made. Reasons for the lack of an appointment are limited only by the creativity of the reluctant partner. "I have too much to do right, now," "I've left numerous messages but the guy never calls me back," and "We are on a waiting-list," are some of he less imaginative evasions I have heard.

How Counseling Works

Counseling often derives its advantages from the simple expedient of having the opportunity to talk, express feelings and be in a situation that encourages listening. Sometimes, there are brilliant flashes of insight, masterful therapeutic maneuvers and clinical genius but most of the time counseling derives its benefit from being able to talk and listen.

Here are the ways that counseling can really work.

---

[53] Unless you have an overall problem with trust and have a paranoid nature in which case you might never trust anybody.

Counseling can be a great sounding board. Only the most arrogant and narcissistic person cannot imagine a different viewpoint that is valuable. Most of us are not completely certain that we are right about everything. All of us, at one time or another, need a reality check, especially for the emotional issues in our life. The more sensitive the issues, the more reality checking we need to do. The counselor is an independent person with knowledge and experience who can put your thoughts and feelings into perspective. Although your friends and relatives might also be able to do this, the fact that they are not independent moderates the value of their particular point of view.

The counselor's office is also a neutral place where you can discuss emotional issues without getting into a fight. This is more important than it may seem at first glance. When couples are faced with contentious issues, they tend to avoid discussion of them because such debate goes nowhere and often ends up in a fight. The result is that these important issue are never discussed and the hostility builds. The counselor's office is a relatively safe place to discuss such issues in that it is a neutral place not associated with hostility and tension. The presence of a third person will provide some break on the emotions although my office has been the setting for some very heated arguments indeed. Moreover, because the session lasts about an hour, the discussion is time-limited. For all these reasons, the therapist's office may be the only place that communication can occur. I will sometimes, give implicit instructions for specific subjects not to be discussed except in my office.

No matter how experienced a therapist is, the only way to really assess a relationship is to watch the couple interact. This was brought home to me some years ago. I had been seeing a man whose marriage was in difficulty. He presented himself as the epitome of reason. His accounts of events painted a picture of a victimized husband, powerless against the emotional outbursts of his wife. I arranged for a joint session so I could see how they interacted. I discovered that his *logical* account of their various positions on important issues was correct. The way he treated her, however, bordered on the abusive. He had accurately portrayed the *content* of the communication but had substantially misrepresented the *form* of it.

An experienced counselor can not only tell you a lot about the state of your relationship by watching you communicate, he or she can begin to restructure your communication pattern within the session. For example, it might be that whenever she talks he avoids eye-contact, or that whenever he talks, she dives in with a comment before he has had a chance to finish. These communication habits have become so automatic that it is difficult for the partners to recognize them. A counselor can begin to change these habits within the sessions.

A good counselor will attempt to provide both parties structured exercises and experiences that will help restore perspective and even help restructure their thoughts and ideas. For example, I was recently working with a couple in which the man had difficulty seeing his wife's point of view, on anything. I played some music, asked them to listen carefully and share their interpretations of it. His interpretation was vastly different from hers - he saw storm clouds, she saw flowers. I then asked him to listen to the music again and see if he could see flowers, or at least understand how someone might make that interpretation. The second time around, with a little goading, he recognized how someone might get the idea of flowers from listening to certain orchestral phrases. It was his first step in recognizing that his partner could reasonably come to a different interpretation of events.

A partner is more likely to accept an interpretation of his or her behavior from a counselor than they are from their spouse. Both partners have very good knowledge of each other and are likely to have some insight into each other's motivation and behavior. At times of stress and hostility, however, partners are not going to listen to each other, regardless of how valid the points may be.

> **You are more likely to accept comments made from a third party like a therapist, even if the comments are the same ones that you have rejected many times when they have come from your partner.**

A counselor is also a better sounding board than a relative or a friend. There is no question that relatives and friends can have useful insights and comments. The problem is that your communication with your friends is likely to be less forthright than it is with a therapist because they are friends and you have a vested interest in keeping them as your friends. It is likely that you will seek out only those closest to you who will endorse your feelings and actions and, from this point of view, friends and close relatives are almost always sympathetic. Moreover, you run the risk of boring and/or alienating your friends if you are continually moaning to them about your problems. The gossip and intrigue factors fade quickly and you run the risk of losing them altogether.

Index

acceptance, 52, 68, 69, 70, 86, 90
adaptation, 68
addiction, 110
adolescence, 74
adoptees,, 17
AIDS, 44, 112
anger, 7, 27, 40, 48, 50, 52, 53, 59, 63, 64, 66, 77, 79, 85, 88, 89, 92, 98, 99, 102, 103, 107, 110, 113, 115, 117, 128, 129, 130, 134, 150, 151, 152, 153, 155, 156, 158, 162, 163, 164, 165, 166, 171, 172, 173, 176, 177, 182
attachment, 16, 17, 33, 34, 35, 37, 38, 45, 78, 84, 85, 86, 98, 101, 119, 134, 135, 136, 137, 138, 139, 140, 149, 182
Attention Deficit Disorder, 134
attraction, 10, 16, 21, 22, 24, 29, 30, 36, 37, 54, 68, 112, 136
autism, 94, 95, 134
blended families, 15, 54
change, 11, 19, 23, 28, 31, 33, 39, 40, 49, 50, 52, 54, 55, 60, 68, 69, 70, 71, 72, 73, 74, 75, 80, 86, 91, 92, 116, 121, 127, 130, 136, 139, 156, 160, 165, 172, 185
child development, 51
child rearing, 51
childbearing, 21
cognitive restructuring, 165
co-habitation, 48
co-habiting, 46
commitment, 20, 44
communication, 13, 22, 40, 42, 43, 52, 53, 54, 57, 58, 59, 60, 61, 62, 63, 64, 65, 66, 106, 116, 117, 121, 132, 168, 175, 180, 182, 186, 189, 190, 191
Companionship, 18

compromise, 53, 81, 83, 84, 85, 90, 131
Compulsive gambling, 110
conflict, 35, 40, 53, 59, 76, 111, 126, 127, 131, 152, 155, 172
conflict resolution, 53
control, 8, 17, 18, 21, 25, 27, 28, 32, 33, 36, 41, 42, 45, 46, 47, 48, 49, 50, 53, 61, 62, 69, 70, 71, 72, 78, 83, 86, 87, 89, 90, 93, 98, 99, 100, 101, 105, 106, 107, 109, 111, 113, 115, 116, 126, 127, 128, 130, 131, 134, 136, 140, 149, 150, 155, 157, 171, 176, 183, 186
counseling, 11, 34, 51, 80, 82, 97, 102, 123, 183, 184, 185, 188
criticism, 28, 57, 63, 171, 172
dating, 22, 38, 44, 47
delegation, 47
Denial, 88
dependence, 37, 43, 44, 45, 46, 75, 84, 86, 100, 173
depression, 25, 64, 79, 88, 90, 100, 104, 105, 123, 158, 165, 182
divorce, 7, 10, 13, 15, 20, 48, 72, 83, 97, 98, 102, 105, 106, 107, 108, 112, 139, 182, 183, 187
eating disorders, 195
embarrassment, 110, 111, 119
emotional availability, 137, 138
energy, 36, 37, 52, 55, 74, 90, 92, 102, 104, 131, 139
erotic energy, 37
fairness, 48
family history, 19
family traditions, 54
family values, 51
fidelity, 64, 80, 96, 110, 112, 171, 172
fighting, 53

fighting, 53
forgiveness, 9, 75, 76, 101, 113, 116, 158, 159, 165
Freud, 77
frustration, 24, 28, 53, 81, 82, 85, 98, 102, 128, 150, 158, 159, 164, 172
frustration tolerance, 53, 131
gender differences, 64, 83, 123, 137, 149
guilt, 150
habit, 11, 22, 23, 26, 27, 28, 46, 47, 48, 63, 66, 68, 73, 84, 85, 99, 110, 116, 190
Heisenberg, 68
honesty, 51, 110, 111, 112, 113, 117
hormones, 29, 30, 32, 34, 65, 149
hostility, 63, 103, 179, 180, 189, 190
immune system, 74, 123, 124
impulse control, 8, 36, 53, 110, 111, 113
independence, 37, 43, 44, 45, 46, 75, 86, 87, 100, 120, 134
infatuation, 24
influence, 13, 17, 21, 29, 30, 31, 32, 36, 37, 55, 63, 83, 91, 98, 123, 129, 163, 184
integrity, 110, 111
intimacy, 32, 66, 103, 115, 120, 121, 148, 149, 150, 152, 153, 169, 177, 182
jealousy, 54, 84, 115, 126
limited time marriage contract, 19
listening, 57, 58, 62, 131, 137, 148, 180, 183, 188, 190
loss of independence, 44
marital stability, 48
meaning., 6, 51, 90, 123, 167, 170
money, 47
motivation, 14, 27, 30, 62, 77, 78, 97, 190

Novel Erotic Attachment, 32, 33, 38, 45, 144
Novel Erotic Attraction, 69
novelty, 35
nurturing, 14, 37, 52, 54, 101, 139
parental similarity, 22
parenthood, 50
parenting, 15, 16, 19, 37, 50, 52, 81, 99, 135
parenting., 16
patience, 8, 63, 82, 95
personality, 8, 21, 73, 80, 111, 115, 116, 184
pheromones, 30
power, 11, 23, 32, 36, 38, 43, 45, 48, 50, 52, 71, 76, 90, 100, 104, 106, 112, 147, 149, 157
pre-marital counseling, 34
procreation, 9, 14
projection, 40, 62
psychoanalysis, 77
psychotherapy, 135
rejection, 39, 40, 42, 44, 63, 101, 172
resentment, 52
responsibility, 9, 25, 47, 56, 69, 77, 78, 79, 80, 81, 83, 89, 101, 102, 126, 159, 181
romance, 9, 11, 35, 43, 85, 144, 147, 149
Sadness, 89, 90, 92
self-discipline, 8, 81
self-esteem, 23, 67, 81, 100, 101, 121, 180
self-indulgence, 81
self-respect, 53
separateness, 43, 46
separation, 38, 105, 106, 107
sex, 9, 14, 17, 21, 30, 32, 33, 34, 36, 37, 44, 74, 82, 85, 96, 102, 103, 112, 113, 126, 137, 148, 149, 150, 151, 152, 153, 172, 182

sex addicts, 36
sex drive, 74, 137, 182
sexual abuse, 150, 151
sexually transmitted diseases, 14, 44, 112
Shakespeare, 29
Shame, 110
Sharing, 5, 9, 38, 40, 47, 48, 53, 71, 116, 118, 119, 120, 121, 122, 123, 124, 135, 137, 168, 174
stress, 6, 16, 18, 26, 27, 30, 39, 55, 56, 75, 95, 97, 123, 124, 127, 149, 156, 160, 179, 187, 190

support, 6, 15, 16, 84, 124, 139, 155, 157, 159
teamwork, 120
the romantic love myth, 39
time-out, 128
togetherness, 38, 136
tolerance, 53, 55, 69, 82, 95, 180
Trust, 5, 9, 43, 44, 48, 99, 101, 109, 110, 111, 112, 113, 114, 115, 116, 117, 126, 134, 135, 136, 137, 138, 151, 160, 168, 173, 176, 182, 187, 188
unconditional love, 17, 24, 34, 101, 119
wellness, 195

Howard J. Rankin Ph.D is a clinical psychologist with masters and doctoral degrees from the University of London. A clinical psychologist who has been in private practice for twenty-five years, Dr. Rankin has held academic appointments at the universities of London and Oxford and at the University of South Carolina where he is currently an adjunct professor in the School of Public Health.

Dr Rankin has published over fifty scientific papers on addictions and eating disorders and for ten years was the editor of the scientific journal "Addictive Behaviors." In addition to his scientific writing, he has published many articles in the popular media. He was a regular columnist for the European version of Psychology Today and a variety of British magazines before moving to the United States in 1986. Dr. Rankin has written and developed a tape series *Get Motivated Get Smart Get Slim* and *Seven Steps to Wellness* as well as *Ten Steps to a Great Relationship*.

In his clinical practice he was the Chief of the Eating Disorders Unit, St.Andrews Hospital, Northampton, as well as consultant to the drug and alcohol treatment units. His private practice focuses on relationships, eating disorders, stress, depression and trauma. Dr. Rankin is the founder and director of the Carolina Wellness Retreat, a lifestyle change program located on Hilton Head Island, South Carolina.

Dr. Rankin's work has been quoted in the print media in such papers as The Wall Street Journal, The Los Angeles Times, The Baltimore Sun, The Dallas Morning News, The Cleveland Plain Dealer, Newsday and such magazines as Ladies Home Journal, Health, Mademoiselle, New Woman, Weight Watchers and Prevention. He has been a frequent radio and television guest both here and in his native Britain.

For more information for Dr. Rankin's professional activities, including his seminars and workshops, please visit his website at www.howardrankin.com or write to PO Box 4797, Hilton Head Island, SC 29938-4797.

From Dr. Howard J. Rankin...

7 Steps to Wellness

This book shows you how to control your weight and your life! Most people know what they need to do to lose weight, manage stress and stay in shape, but doing it is another matter. In this book, Dr. Rankin shows the 7 Steps that you need to take for optimal health and performance.

Learn how to...

- *Capture motivation - and maintain it*

- *Develop self-management skills*

- *Learn how to develop positive thinking*

- *Develop self-control*

- *Defeat bingeing*

- *Cope with high risks*

- *Get the support you want.*

Comes with nutrition and exercise guide, 14 day meal plan, daily journal and eating-out guide. Available from bookstores or by calling (803) 842-7797

ISBN 0-9658261-1-2   **Price $11.95**

From Dr. Howard J. Rankin...

Get Motivated Get Smart Get Slim!

This original tape series includes some of the material of *7 Steps to Wellness* on six audiotapes,. Narrated by the author, the tapes include sections on motivation, self-management, mindfulness, bingeing, temptation management, coping and dealing with others. It also includes motivational link exercises and imagery with realistic sounds which really help to reprogram your key associations.

A bonus tape includes "A Personal Message," designed to help you through the day and keep motivation high.

As well as the 14 day menu plan, the nutrition and exercise guides, the Personal healthscope and Dining-out guide come in handy, wallet-size booklets. There are also motivational stickers to keep you focused on your goals!

Get Motivated Get Smart Get Slim is available by calling 803-842-7797

We are on the Internet! Visit us at the following locations..

www.relationships_steps.com
Look here for information about *10 Step to a Great Relationship*. The site contains news about updates and other related products as well as seminars, workshops and retreats.

www.wellness_steps.com
This site contains information about the book *7 Steps to Wellness*. It, too, contains information about updates, new products, seminars, workshops and retreats.

www.communication_steps.com
This site contains information about workshops and seminars for professionals. Includes information on the continuing education programs on communication for health-related and other professionals.

www.motivation_steps.com
This site contains information on the *Get Motivated Get Smart Get Slim* program. It also includes information about motivation seminars and workshops.

www.howardrankin.com
This site provides information about Dr. Howard J. Rankin, Howard J. Rankin & Associates Inc., and Stepwise Press Inc., including professional activities and publications.